DEFUSING THE ANGRY PATRON

A How-To-Do-It Manual for Librarians and Paraprofessionals

Rhea Joyce Rubin

**HOW-TO-DO-IT MANUALS
FOR LIBRARIANS**

NUMBER 100

NEAL-SCHUMAN PUBLISHERS, INC.
New York, London

Published by Neal-Schuman Publishers, Inc.
100 Varick Street
New York, NY 10013

The paper used in this publication meets the minimum requirements of American National Standard for Information Sciences—Permanence of Paper for Printed Library Materials, ANSI Z39.48–1992.

Printed and bound in the United States of America.

ISBN 1–55570–372–0

Library of Congress Cataloging-in-Publication Data

Rubin, Rhea Joyce.
    Defusing the angry patron : a how-to-do-it manual for librarians
and paraprofessionals / Rhea Joyce Rubin.
        p. cm. — (How to-do-it manuals for librarians ; no. 100)
    Includes bibliographical references and index.
    ISBN 1–55570–372–0
    1. Libraries and readers—United States.   2. Customer services—United States.
    3. Anger—United States.   I. Title.   II. How-to-do-it manuals for libraries ; no. 100.

Z711.R79   2000
025.5—dc21   99–048199

This book is dedicated to Hannah, my sweet and artistic daughter, upon graduating from high school; and to Sandy, my favorite ALA roommate, upon changing careers.

CONTENTS

ACKNOWLEDGMENTS

Defusing the Angry Patron has been in the making for a long time. I am grateful to all the people who contributed anecdotes and examples for it. Many "contributors" had no idea that their stories would end up in print because they were shared in workshops I've given in forty states during the past nineteen years.

Recently I have had the good fortune to work with paraprofessional associations in Illinois and California, individual libraries and library systems in California, and the staff of the Chicago Public Library. My thanks to them all and to Kathleen Weibel, Director of Staff Development at the Chicago Public Library.

I'd also like to express my appreciation to three people who were essential to my finishing *Defusing the Angry Patron*. Janet Turman, previously of the Berkeley Public Library, helped me by critiquing my workshops, sharing her own stuff, and reading this book in draft. Charles Harmon, Director of Publishing for Neal-Schuman Publishers, Inc., encouraged me to publish this work as a How-to-Do-it Manual and rewarded my decision by both editing it and rushing it into print. And it was Pat Schuman who got me hooked on writing by editing and publishing my first book in 1975 as a Neal-Schuman imprint of Oryx Press.

As usual, I couldn't have written this in my spare time without my staff and family's help. Lars, the computer maven, set me up on a new laptop so I could work in hotel rooms. Schmoop Enterprises provided security and entertainment, sometimes simultaneously. My husband, Larry, made sure I didn't go the "all work and no play" route. And our wonderful daughter, Hannah, to whom this is dedicated, shared her concern and common sense as I decided the future of this manuscript.

PREFACE

The so-called "problem patron" is the focus of many books, videos, and articles. My feeling is that it is time to eliminate "problem patron" from our collective vocabulary. Yes, libraries have their share of vandals, flashers, and people who smell bad. And some libraries have had to deal with gunfire and deaths on their premises. But rarely is it the person, or *only* the person, who is the difficulty. Instead, the situations that patrons present may be (or may become) problems for us. The overwhelming majority of these difficult situations involve an angry patron.

The reason that angry patrons present serious dilemmas for library staff is that anger is contagious. Talking with—and listening to—an angry person can take a personal toll on staff who may feel angry, frustrated, and/or helpless. Staff may feel like victims in their own libraries.

This book is for all library staff members who:

- are sick and tired of being yelled at by patrons;
- aren't sure what to do when someone looks angry;
- just want to get on with their jobs;
- are frightened by the unexpected high emotion over a simple library transaction;
- are angry themselves because they feel dumped on by the public; and,
- feel frustrated that they lose their cool under pressure.

We do not need to feel powerless in the face of anger. We can take control of the situation and feel better about ourselves while, at the same time, calming the patron, solving the presenting problem, and moving on to assist the next patron.

This book is not primarily about behavior that threatens the public safety or interferes with others' use of the library's services, although some of these situations are addressed. In most cases, such behavior is illegal and must be settled with the assistance of the police. This book *is* about the everyday occurrence we all dread: the patron who is upset about a library policy or procedure and vents his or her anger on staff.

Direct and practical, this book will:

- put anger into context,
- use real library situations,
- offer various techniques (so you can find the one that's comfortable for you),

- present scripts as examples from which you can create your own,
- give exercises so you can practice your new skills,
- suggest methods to release your own stress and anger, and,
- provide tools to use on the job.

Defusing the Angry Patron is meant to be a workbook rather than a textbook. The first chapter, "A Primer on Anger," summarizes anger research that points to methods for dealing with this difficult emotion. The chapter includes an exercise designed to help you consider your own actions when you are angry and your reactions when confronted with an angry person. To make the most of what you read, take the time to do this exercise and the others that appear throughout the book.

"Preventive Measures" is the next chapter. It suggests actions which can minimize the number of angry patrons you see. Some of these are things you as an individual can do, such as welcoming patrons as they arrive; others are for the library as an institution to do, such as signage. Included is a discussion of the expectations and attitudes of patrons and of staff.

"How To Do It" is the heart of the manual. It presents twenty basic strategies for defusing anger in a patron or any other human being (i.e., co-worker, friend, or relative). Exercises are given so you can practice these strategies to see which ones "fit" you best. Of course some will feel more natural and will work better for you than others. Try them out! Perhaps the most important technique for calming an upset person is to listen carefully. So the following chapter is dedicated to listening skills. As in the rest of the book, I encourage you to create your own responses rather than to memorize these.

"Beyond the Basics" addresses difficult situations which are different from, yet similar to, dealing with anger. Complaints, accusations, and unacceptable behaviors are discussed. Telephone situations are introduced, too.

The last two chapters are focused on you rather than the patron. "Coping With Your Own Anger" suggests ways of letting go of the stress and emotion we so often pick up from people who are angry. "Help Is At Hand" offers practical tools for you to use when coping with angry patrons.

At the end of each chapter is a summary. You can use this to review what you have read or to share major points with a co-worker or friend. A bibliography and index complete the book.

I first started working with angry patrons as a jail librarian in the 1970s. My angry patrons included both inmates and correctional officers who were quick to anger and difficult to reason with. Public libraries asked me to help their staffs learn techniques for coping with animosity and so began the twenty-five-year path to this book. Besides my own experiences, *Defusing the Angry Patron* reflects the comments and experiences of thousands of public and college librarians who have attended my workshops on the topic.

Feel free to contact me with your own stories and techniques. I can be reached via Neal-Schuman Publishers or at rjrubin@ix. netcom.com.

1 A PRIMER ON ANGER

WHAT IS ANGER?

Of all the many human emotions, anger is the one we most often deal with in a "problem" situation in the library. A regular patron refuses to pay a fine, a pillar of the community throws a book when told that it cannot be renewed, a student shouts obscenities about the policy on reference materials, or a paragon of respectability refuses to let anyone else use the Internet terminal. What is going on? Their behavior tells us that they are angry. But what *is* anger?

A PROTECTIVE MECHANISM

People become angry in order to protect themselves when they are under a lot of stress. Sociologists and psychologists theorize that daily life has become so stressful that "free-floating" frustration is common. Meanwhile, our fast-paced society has become accustomed to instant gratification—one-hour cleaners, half-hour film developing, and fast-food drive-through windows are old news in an age where E-mail and ATMs are prevalent. The combination of daily stress and high expectations leads to frustration when anything moves slowly or goes wrong. Then a person focuses all of her pent-up ire on the immediate cause. So, waiting in line at the reference desk may produce an angry outburst disproportionate to the situation. Although it's small consolation when you are the target of anger, *all* service positions are feeling this society-wide problem. Banks, airlines, and retail outlets all report an increase in expressed anger.

The two most common ways to protect oneself in response to stress and conflict are *avoidance* and *dominance*. These are sometimes called the "flight or fight" response, which humans share with animals. In order to avoid conflict, or to end a confrontation quickly, most people flee the situation (avoidance) or fight to win (dominance). An angry person avoiding a situation may actually leave or may withdraw into silence; this flight response is passive. An angry person who wants to dominate may yell or show aggressive physical behavior such as pounding the desk; this fight style is aggressive. Neither the submissive nor the dominant person is willing to look for a mutual solution. What is really needed is for one person to adopt a third response: problem solving. This will be discussed more fully under *Be Assertive* in Chapter 3.

One way to defuse anger is to lower the stress level. For example, people while at a picnic do not anger as easily as the same people

1

would in the employment application line. For the library this means that the more comfortable and pleasant we make the general atmosphere, the less likely we will witness uncontrolled anger. Similarly, if we assist the patron in decreasing his defensiveness, we can minimize the chance of anger. For example, if staff explains that *all* new cardholders are limited in the number of books they may check out, the patron may not take it personally and become angry.

A SECONDARY EMOTION

Anger is often a mask over another emotion; that is, anger is the visible emotion (called the secondary emotion) that develops in response to another (the primary) feeling. This is significant to us, because one way to handle anger is to discover and deal with the primary emotion. Usually the primary feeling is a loss of self-esteem, so we can dissipate the anger by increasing self-esteem, trust, or pride.

You do not need to be a psychiatrist or social worker to do this. You can increase patrons' self-esteem simply by treating them courteously. It is a truism that everyone deserves respect; more important is the fact that every individual *feels* that she *deserves* respect. And when she doesn't get it, anger may surface. For example, if a professor is irritated while using the college library, a staff member can help the situation by addressing the patron as "doctor." By doing this, the staff person demonstrates respect, boosting the professor's self-esteem and thereby lessening the chance of anger.

Other common emotions masked by anger are embarrassment and fear. Let's look at some examples. A regular patron may be embarrassed when told he has an overdue fine or may feel that the library is not showing him due respect. By calling the patron by name and acknowledging his status as a frequent patron, the circulation staff member may be able to defuse any anger. Or the patron may be embarrassed in front of you and family members or friends accompanying him about not having enough money on hand; by explaining that he can pay the fine next time, the staff person can eliminate that discomfort. Another possibility is that the patron is afraid, perhaps, of losing his borrowing privileges. With young patrons, especially, there can be a real fear that the parents will get angry. By allowing the person to still check out some materials, the staff person can defuse both of these situations.

Anger can also mask feelings of guilt. Ironically, some people feel guilty for feeling angry and then feel resentful of the object of the anger (i.e., you) for making them feel guilty. A patron can sometimes be calmed just by acknowledging the difficult situation because that awareness alleviates the sense of guilt. For example, if a patron has waited in a long, slow line to reach the circulation desk a staff person

"No man is angry that feels not himself hurt." Francis Bacon

can help an angry patron calm down by agreeing that waiting in line is frustrating. Ditto with trying to use a broken photocopier.

You can tell that anger is a secondary emotion by how quickly it disappears and is replaced by another feeling, especially when new information is introduced. For example, a high school student may be angry to find someone else using her carrel; the person feels ownership of that desk—overlooking the square—where she studies every day and feels that she "deserves" that window seat. When shown that a new row of carrels has been installed closer to the window, the patron no longer cares about her customary desk because she now has a better view (which she "deserves").

| EXERCISE | **SELF-TEST** |

I. Think about the last time a patron—or anyone else—expressed anger *at you.*

1. Who was the person?

2. How did you know s/he was angry at you?

3. What did s/he say to you?

4. What did s/he do?

5. How did you respond? Check all that apply:
   ___ Yelled back   ___ Magnified the situation
   ___ Gave an ultimatum   ___ Used sarcasm
   ___ Walked away   ___ Minimized the situation
   ___ Cried   ___ Took it personally
   ___ Called police prematurely   ___ Grew silent
   ___ Felt guilty   ___ Other (what?):

6. How did you feel during the interaction? Check all that apply:
   ___ Angry   ___ Defensive
   ___ Frightened   ___ Misunderstood
   ___ Nervous   ___ Guilty
   ___ Why me?   ___ Powerful
   ___ Frustrated   ___ Powerless
   ___ Pressured   ___ Other (what?):

7. How did you feel afterwards?
   ___ Angry   ___ Guilty
   ___ Exhausted   ___ Sorry
   ___ Vengeful   ___ Embarrassed
   ___ Nauseated   ___ Trembly
   ___ Other:

8. Other memories/ comments:

SELF-TEST — *Continued*

II. Let's look at the flip side of the situation. Remember a recent time when *you* expressed anger at a friend, coworker, or relative.

1. Who was the person?

2. What did you say?

3. What did you do during the interaction? Check all that apply:
   ___ Screamed   ___ Used sarcasm
   ___ Cried   ___ Pounded or threw something
   ___ Exaggerated   ___ Name called
   ___ Made demands   ___ Mind read
   ___ Other (what?)

4. What did you do after the interaction? Check all that apply:
   ___ Cried   ___ Ate
   ___ Pouted   ___ Threw up
   ___ Other (what?)

5. How did you feel afterwards? Check all that apply.
   ___ Relieved   ___ Proud
   ___ Victorious   ___ Embarrassed
   ___ Defensive   ___ Apologetic
   ___ Still angry   ___ Guilty
   ___ Disgusted   ___ Nauseated
   ___ Other (what?)

6. Other memories/comments:

WHAT WE KNOW MAY NOT MATTER

All of us who work in libraries value knowledge. But information alone may not be useful with an angry patron. This is because people do not act on what they *know*. People act on how they *feel* about what they know. So even a library board member who knows all the policies may act angry when a staff person expects him to obey the rules—again the person may feel that the staff person is not showing him respect.

Feelings can be altered by a change in perception that may be based on additional knowledge. So a person who is angry that someone behind her in line has stepped on her foot may calm immediately upon seeing that it is a blind person behind her. That piece of information changes her perception that affects the anger. This explains why giving a patron a context for the situation may be helpful. It also demonstrates one way we can keep from getting angry at patrons—by seeing the situation differently (e.g., understanding that the patron is embarrassed) we avoid anger.

A PHYSIOLOGICAL RESPONSE

Extreme anger has many physiological components. Typically there is tension in the muscles, chest, or head (which can cause headaches), shallow and difficult breathing, and heavy perspiration. Digestion stops, causing stomach aches. The heart rate increases, blood pressure rises, and adrenaline flows.

These physical outcomes lead many to consider frequent anger a health problem. Remember all the interest in the 1970s with "Type A" personalities who are prone to both outbursts of anger and to heart attacks? There is much dispute over which is more medically dangerous: habitually suppressing anger (which may lead to depression) or habitually expressing anger (which may lead to heart attacks). The consensus seems to be that anger should be managed through appropriate communication, neither explosion nor implosion. (See more on this in Chapter 6.)

Perhaps the most interesting physiological response from our point of view is the increased circulation of sugar-enriched blood *away* from the brain. The enhanced blood moves toward the limbs to prepare to fight or flee. The brain is getting less blood than usual so that it is nearly impossible for the furious person to think and act rationally. Have you heard the expression "I was so angry I couldn't think straight"? The angry person must be calmed down before she is presented with rational solutions to a problem.

ANGER'S SIBLINGS

It is essential to differentiate between normal anger—which can be assuaged with techniques in this book—and two of its siblings.

Anger is *not* hostility, which is an attitude characterized by dislike, distrust, envy, or antagonism. Library staff probably cannot reduce hostility because it is an underlying attitude—a long-term predilection taught or reinforced by others—and not an emotional response. Some public library branches or small special libraries report that they have had an impact on a patron's hostility; by consistently exhibiting patience they have taught the patron to expect a positive atmosphere and so he knows the library is a place to relax and stay calm.

How can you tell if a person is hostile rather than angry? By noting a pattern of repeated negative behavior and speech. Keeping track of patrons' behavior (as discussed in Chapter 3) allows staff to see the patterns that demonstrate hostility.

Anger is *not* aggression, which is an action toward another with the intention of doing harm. Aggression implies intentionally harmful behavior, which is against the law. Aggression is easier to identify than hostility because the nature of the behavior speaks for itself. You are not responsible for handling belligerent patrons; security staff or local police should be called in to these situations.

One last word on what anger is not: some physical and emotional disabilities can cause people to appear angry or difficult when in fact they are not. Here are some examples:

- a person with diabetes whose blood sugar is too high or too low may seem drunk
- a person with autism may seem to be on drugs
- a person with a traumatic head injury may act aggressively or seem to be hostile (e.g., asking the same questions repeatedly due to memory loss)
- a person who is a paranoid schizophrenic may be highly verbal and delusional and make unreasonable accusations
- a person with mental illness who is off her medication schedule may seem to be on drugs

Look at the patron's neck and wrist to see if he's wearing a medi-alert emblem; this can be a significant clue that illness, disability, or medication is the underlying problem. If you suspect that the patron has a disability that is causing the behavior in question, stay calm and consult with a supervisor before taking other action.

The dictionary is full of synonyms for "anger" because it comes in so many forms. The difference between "frustrated" and "furious" is really only one of degree. The angrier the person, the higher the heat in the thermometer on the following page. The higher the heat, the

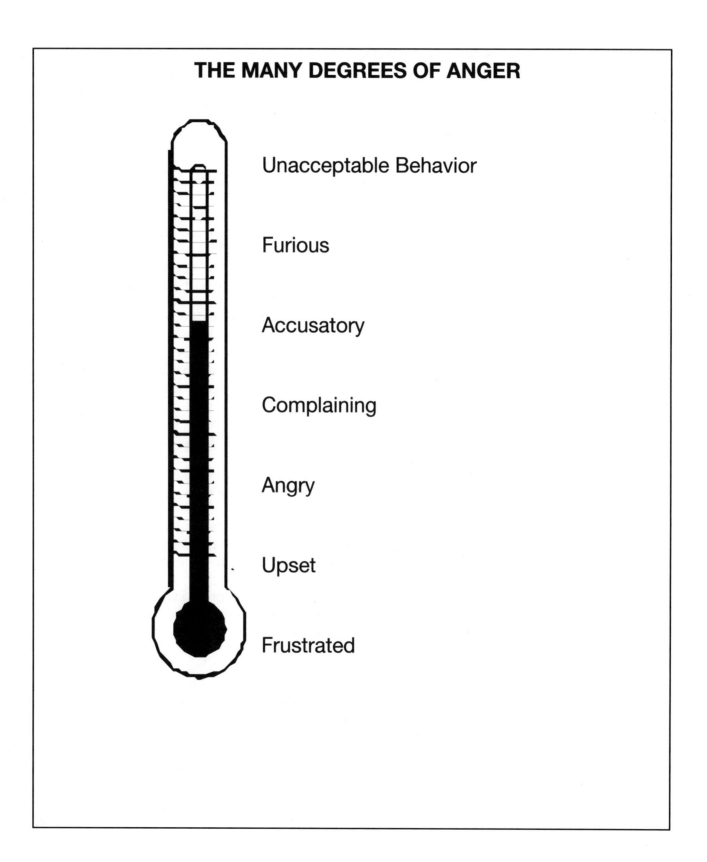

THE MANY DEGREES OF ANGER

Unacceptable Behavior

Furious

Accusatory

Complaining

Angry

Upset

Frustrated

"Anger blows out the lamp of the mind." Robert Green Ingersoll

more intense the conflict. The more intense, the more we tend to personalize it and escalate the situation.

In this book we will discuss all of these degrees of anger and present approaches for dealing with each of them. Whatever technique is used, it is essential to separate yourself personally from your role as the library's representative. Never take the anger personally or you double the work; if you are angry too, you have two angry people to calm down! As my colleague Janet Turman says, "Take it professionally, not personally."

Anger has been likened to a raging fire that needs oxygen to keep it burning. You can decide whether or not to be that second source of oxygen.

SUMMARY

- Anger is a *protective mechanism* resulting from stress. To defuse anger, we need to lower the patron's stress level.
- Anger is a *secondary emotion* masking some other feeling, usually a loss of self-esteem, embarrassment, or fear. To dissipate anger we need to respond to the primary emotion.
- People do not act on what they know, but on how they *feel* about what they know. So the patron's feelings are paramount in any exchange.
- Anger causes blood to flow *away* from the brain and so an angry person does not think rationally. To solve the patron's problem we must allow time for blood to return to the brain.
- Hostility and aggression are *not* the same thing as anger and cannot be managed with the same techniques.
- Some disabilities can mimic difficult behavior.
- The more intense the anger, the more likely we are to personalize it and become angry in response. Don't take the patron's anger personally.

2 PREVENTIVE MEASURES

Most patrons enter library transactions in a calm and civilized manner. If they become angry patrons it is because one or more expectations were not met. Other patrons arrive at the library in a frustrated or irate mood; one look at their faces and you can tell that you have ready-made angry patrons. In both cases we can take preventive measures to keep contented patrons calm and to refrain from escalating a frustrated patron into fury.

These preventive measures are known as good customer service. If staff acts positively and proactively with patrons, most patrons can be satisfied and most confrontations avoided. Patrons are satisfied when they feel that both the quality of the tangibles (e.g., books, buildings, information, programs) and the service are excellent. Of the two (tangibles and service), service is usually the most important to customers. For example, a recent library study demonstrated that patrons who found the material they needed and were treated efficiently and politely by circulation staff rated the library as "satisfactory" while patrons at the same library who had the identical experience—*except* that the staff member smiled at them—rated the library as "excellent" (Leland, 1995).

WELCOMING BEHAVIORS

Many library users find the library intimidating and its classification systems and rules difficult. Adult new readers, people with English as a second language, newcomers who are not accustomed to public libraries, or people who have had unpleasant experiences in other libraries all may be uncomfortable at your library. Their discomfort can manifest itelf in ways that are difficult for staff.

Research on stress among library staff found that patrons were the major source of stress; however, patrons were also the most commonly cited source of satisfaction to library workers.

Other patrons come to the library already upset; staff can recognize it all the way across the room in the tightness in the patron's face and other nonverbal signals. (See more on this later in this chapter.) Perhaps a mother, still dressed in a work suit and heels, with all her children in tow, stops in at the library so that one child can get a book for an unexpected homework assignment. Or a teen, anxious and clearly embarrassed, approaches the desk to ask for health information. Whatever the reason for the patron's stress, staff can escalate it or reduce it by their behavior. When patrons feel welcome in the library—sense that they will be helped and feel invited to ask questions—they relax and are no longer candidates for angry scenes.

Try these welcoming behaviors:

- Acknowledge people in line. Let the patron know that you see him waiting. You can do this by saying "I'll be right with you" or "I'll be with you in just a minute" or "Thank you for waiting." Alternatively, you can simply smile or nod to show that you are aware of his presence. As the saying goes, "You only have one chance to make a first impression."
- Greet each patron in a respectful and friendly manner. Some staff use standard greetings such as "Good morning" or "Hello." Others move right to service with "How can I help you?"
- Use the patron's name if you know it. There are a few caveats to this suggestion, though. Do not call a patron by name if the person is asking a confidential question or if you are giving private information (e.g., overdue fines) when other patrons can hear. Avoid using the patron's name if you do not know how to pronounce it. And don't use the patron's name if staff do not wear nametags; it can seem rude or condescending for only one side of the conversation to be on a personal name basis.
- Listen carefully and give the patron your full attention.
- Make eye contact with the patron. "Soft focus" eye contact is the term for looking directly at a person without staring. You can do this by looking at the face in general—the forehead or chin—rather than straight into the person's eyes. Although it is tempting to continue with paperwork, or to look at the computer screen, people do not feel as if they have your attention unless you look at them.
- Maintain a polite tone of voice and body language.
- Alter your nonverbal cues as necessary so that they are congruent with the patron's demeanor. The more similar your nonverbal communication is to the other person's, the more likely she will consider you welcoming and nonthreatening. For example, if you and the patron are on the same physical level (sitting or standing) and if you both are smiling or looking serious.
- Use words the patron understands and avoid library jargon. Few people other than library staff know what "ILL" means or what an "OPAC" is.
- Be proactive—ask how you can help and offer assistance beyond what is requested. A simple form of this is to ask each patron "Is there anything else I can help you with?" at the end of the transaction. Adopting a trick from retail businesses, some libraries now have staff members approach library patrons on the floor or in the stacks to ask "Are you finding what you need?" or "Can I help you find anything?"

POSITIVE APPROACH AND LANGUAGE

Being positive means stressing what you and the library can do for the patron rather than what you cannot do. Speaking positively conveys the message that the library wants to satisfy the patron and that staff are there to help. Often staff members respond to a request by saying, "We don't do that" or "I can't do that" instead of emphasizing what the library can do.

For example, a patron who asks to take a reference book out overnight probably hears "You can't check out reference books." (Note that "reference books" is another example of library jargon.) Instead the staff person could respond with "Let's find a copy of this book which you can take out; this copy doesn't leave the library." Another common example is the staff person who says "That's not my job" or "I can't do that" in response to a request. Instead the staff member might say "Let me take you to someone who can do that for you." Below are some more examples.

A recent study showed that when 100 people do not return to a business or service, 68% of them state that the reason was rude or indifferent staff behavior.

When You'd Say	Try This Instead
I can't . . .	I can . . .
It's not our policy . . .	Usually we . . .
You're wrong . . .	My understanding . . .
We don't . . .	We do . . .
You have to . . .	It would help if you . . .
We never . . .	Today . . .
You don't understand . . .	Let me clarify . . .
I'm not allowed to . . .	The best way I can help . . .
You can't . . .	You can . . .
I don't know . . .	I'll find out . . .
I have no idea . . .	I know who can help . . .

EXERCISE

Add some examples from your library:

-
-
-
-

NONVERBAL LANGUAGE

Social scientists state that only 7 percent of a message is conveyed through words alone; nonverbal language accounts for the rest. Facial expressions and gestures are the types of nonverbal language we are usually most aware of. But nonverbal communication also includes:

- environmental cues;
- spatial cues;
- physical appearance;
- body motion;
- touch;
- posture;
- eye contact;
- paralanguage; and
- behavior.

Environmental cues relate to the physical surroundings and their look. The types of furnishings and the signage, for example, speak loudly about the library. Is your library comfortable and well lit, with good signage? If so, it sends a welcoming message.

All the other types of nonverbal communication are the direct responsibility of the people involved. The cues are two-way. That is, we react to the nonverbal messages sent by patrons just as they interpret staff members' nonverbal cues. Facial expressions and gestures are widely considered universal but, in fact, they are culturally determined. For example, Americans smile at strangers as a way of showing friendliness and signaling good intentions or agreement. In most Asian countries, however, smiling at a stranger is considered rude and a smile between patron and staff may only signal embarrassment. Another example is the "okay" sign made with the thumb and forefinger. Although this gesture is accepted in the United States, it means "money" in Japan and "zero" in France.

Only 7% of a message is conveyed in words. Body language conveys 55% and paralanguage the other 38%.

The most common spatial cue is the distance people leave between themselves and others. For instance, police officers are routinely taught to be intimidating by moving in to less than a foot from a person's face; this tactic is where the expression "in your face" comes from. The amount of space necessary for a person to feel comfortable (the so-called "comfort zone") is related to the social relationship (e.g., family members stand closer to one another than do strangers) and to the culture. The average American stands comfortably about two and a half feet from another person he knows socially and under two feet from a person known intimately. In Asia, most people stand further apart from strangers; in Europe people stand closer. The next time you are at an international airport terminal, watch the people waiting and note how the personal space they have created relates directly to their country of origin. Even among Americans there are pronounced differences. African-American colleagues, for example, stand closer to one another than do Caucasian coworkers.

Physical appearance includes personal grooming habits as well as clothing and hair styles and neatness. Body motion (e.g., swaying or foot tapping), touch, posture (e.g., leaning toward another or standing with hands on the hips), and eye contact are all personal practices. Our own habits are so ingrained that we are usually unconscious of them—but we notice and interpret or judge them in others.

Paralanguage refers to all the qualities of our speech: pitch, tone of voice, inflection, rate, and volume. We all know how different even a simple sentence can sound if the stress is on one word rather than another, if it's spoken fast or slow, in a whisper or in a shout. For example try repeating aloud the following simple sentence, stressing the word in italics.

You can't borrow magazines.
You *can't* borrow magazines.
You can't *borrow* magazines.
You can't borrow *magazines*.

Your vocal qualities can help you with angry patrons. To calm someone who is irate, speak at a similar rate (speed) as the patron, in the lower end of your pitch scale, and watch your tone of voice. Even the most carefully chosen words can sound hostile if presented antagonistically, and imperfect wording can be okay if your delivery style is positive. Observe others when they are talking with angry people. Do they sound annoyed, impatient, or condescending? These messages are sent by paralanguage.

All nonverbal communication conveys attitude and is interpreted and reacted to as such. Think of the difference between being greeted by a smile from a seated person whose open hands are resting on the

Tone of voice conveys 86% of the conversation over the phone. Words convey the other 14%.

desk and a scowl from a standing person whose fingers are tapping the desk. Or a seated person, looking at a computer screen, who mumbles "hmm?" in your direction. Most people interpret nonverbal behavior different from their own to be hostile, so matching the patron's nonverbal cues can be helpful in defusing an angry patron.

Staff body language that is defensive, suspicious, or judgmental can anger patrons, especially ones who are already frustrated. Crossing your arms on your chest, furrowing your brow, placing your hands on your hips, shaking your head, or wagging your forefinger are examples of such defensive or judgmental body language. Expressing frustration through body language can also upset patrons. Typical nonverbal signals of frustration are short breaths, sighing, clenched hands, or wringing your hands. Rolling your eyes shows impatience and appears condescending. Conversely, staff body language can convey positive attitudes. For example, you can signal openness by leaning forward or standing up in greeting. Supportiveness can be communicated by nodding as the patron speaks or by smiling.

Nonverbal cues from patrons can help you anticipate their needs. For example, the patron who repeatedly checks her watch while waiting in line is clearly concerned about time. When it is her turn for your attention you may skip greetings and move right to giving assistance. Another example is the patron who displays his nervousness by fidgeting, rubbing his hands through his hair repeatedly, and clearing his throat often. When he reaches the desk you may want to be especially friendly in your greeting, taking a moment to say "hello" and to smile.

A few extra words on that common nonverbal signal—the smile— are unfortunately necessary. Some chain grocery stores that require their checkers to smile at customers have reported that some male customers misunderstand the smiles from females, misinterpreting them as invitations. Newspaper articles on the subject have made many library staff members shy about smiling at patrons. This is one area in which each staff person must make a personal judgment call. If you feel uncomfortable smiling at strangers—for whatever reason—then don't do it. A nod can be a suitable substitute as can non-smiling soft focus eye contact.

POLICIES AND PROCEDURES

More often than not, the library's policies and procedures inadvertently trigger a patron's unexpected anger. Library staff work on the boundary between the patron and the library administration and regulations. Staff have to explain conflicting, rigid, outdated, or clumsy procedures to frustrated patrons.

Often libraries have policies and procedures that have built up over time. Perhaps they were thoughtful and appropriate originally but have been amended numerous times as conditions and conventions change. Are the policies still relevant? Look at your library's policies and procedures and ask yourself: "Is this customer-friendly?" If the policy is protective of the library rather than proactive for the patron, is there a compelling reason? For instance, is it necessary to restrict patrons to only three books at a time? Many libraries are revisiting sacrosanct rules governing overdue fines and (lack of) eating in the library to see if they are truly essential for the library's operations. And, if they are not, rewriting the policies.

The library's policies should reflect the library values, mission, and principles. The procedures, in turn, should carry out the policies in practice. So, if a library has a mission to serve all the town's residents, the policy and procedures for obtaining a library card should not be draconian. If a library states that it values access to information, the policy and procedures for using interlibrary loan should make such access easy and inexpensive.

EXERCISE

What examples can you think of where your library's philosophy and procedures are out of sync?

-

-

-

-

Does your library have a mechanism for reporting to administration when you find an instance such as this? What is it?

-

-

-

-

SIGNAGE

Some libraries, borrowing from the retail sector, are using signs to prevent certain common frustrations in patrons. For example, posting signs that:

- alert patrons to the loan periods and any unusual loan rules such as fee-per-use items.
- list items patron needs to speed up circulation or application. "Please have your library card out and ready" or "Please have two forms of identification such as driver's license and . . . "
- apologize for delays and prepare the patron for them. "Thanks for your patience. We will help you as soon as possible" or "The computer is down. All transactions are being done by hand. We are sorry for the inconvenience."

Of course all libraries should have patron behavior policies and library hours posted too.

STAFF ATTITUDES

The dictionary definition of *attitude* is a state of mind, influenced by feelings, thoughts, and tendencies toward certain behavior. But *attitude* also carries a slightly different connotation; when someone says "she sure has an Attitude" we know the reference is to something unpleasant. Unfortunately, library staff (and everyone else) have both kinds of attitudes and display them at work.

Here are some examples: The reference librarian who thinks "Kids are a pain in the neck" as a ten year old approaches the desk. Or the circulation assistant who thinks "Oh, no, it's Mr. Garcia; he's always a grouch." Or the page who thinks "It's not my fault if these books are out of order since I wasn't even here yesterday." All of these library employees are demonstrating negative attitudes by labeling, avoiding responsibility, and placing blame.

If you find yourself falling into habitual negative thoughts about patrons and work, try these approaches:

- Assume good intentions on the part of the patron
- Focus on now, not on past situations
- Try goodwill
- Use empathy; try to see from the patron's point of view
- Focus on positive outcomes
- Examine your prejudices toward groups of people and styles of presentation

EXERCISE

Negative feelings and prejudices usually show up in our language or our body language and the patron can sense it. As the bumper-sticker says "The attitude you send out is usually the one you get back." What negative attitudes do you know you or your coworkers bring to work?

-
-
-
-
-
-
-

STAFF TRAINING

One way to assist staff in changing and monitoring their attitudes and to teach staff new techniques for defusing anger is training. All staff members who interact with the public—from the janitor and the page to the substitute circulation clerk, the reference librarian, and the library director—should have ongoing training. Training topics should include:

- customer service;
- listening skills;
- library security;
- communication skills;
- telephone behavior;
- cross-cultural communication; and
- anger management.

PATRON EXPECTATIONS

Exemplary customer service is defined as fulfilling—or exceeding—customers' expectations. So we must know what their expectations are. Libraries that focus on customer service do periodic user surveys to ascertain the wishes of their patrons. Some common library expectations are:

- ease of use;
- competent staff;
- accurate information;
- availability of desired materials;
- private and confidential transactions;
- safe, quiet facility; and
- patient, courteous, and helpful staff.

Depending on the library and its location and clientele, users might expect:

- bilingual staff;
- unlimited loan periods;
- materials in many languages;
- 24-hour remote access;
- convenient parking;
- cutting-edge technology;
- homework help for school-age children; and
- books by mail.

It seems that it is increasingly difficult to meet expectations. In part this is because of the "tyranny of the urgent" which has created an expectation of immediate service available twenty-four hours a day. For example, overnight mail was superseded by fax and then by e-mail for instant response. Another reason it is difficult to meet expectations is that consumers do not always state, or even consciously know, how much they expect. A telling study by the FAA in 1999

EXERCISE

What are some other expectations your users have for your library?

-
-
-
-

showed that the airlines had no fatalities at all in 1998, and fewer lost bags than in previous years, but the airlines received more complaints than ever before. If people expected only to get where they were going safely and with their luggage, they should have been pleased. But they expected more than that; they wanted delicious food, comfortable seats, pleasant flight attendants, and on-time arrivals.

The irony is that people can use the library, not receive what they say they want (e.g., a certain book) and still leave satisfied, but only if their other expectations—especially of good customer service from friendly proactive staff—are met. This is why customer service can be seen as preventing angry customers: if none of a patron's expectations are met, she will be frustrated. But if the service from staff meets or exceeds expectations, the empty-handed patron may still leave the library smiling.

PATRON FEEDBACK

One realistic patron expectation is that his opinions are valued. In order to convey the library's interest in hearing from patrons, many libraries provide suggestion boxes in the library and/or on the library Web page or catalog. It is essential that the library administration respond to every comment in the suggestion box or the library belies its intended purpose and sends the message that patron responses are not welcomed.

In addition to suggestion boxes, libraries may use feedback forms. Feedback forms are similar to complaint forms except they encourage not only negative but positive comments. Often they ask specific questions of the patrons rather than the open-ended question posed by a blank card. Applause forms, used by some hotel chains, specifically elicit compliments from patrons. Library staff as well as patrons should be encouraged to use suggestion or applause forms.

Periodic user surveys, of course, are also a valuable vehicle for patron response and essential to keeping the library focused on its community's needs.

SUMMARY

In order to keep contented patrons calm and to refrain from escalating a frustrated patron into anger, try the following tips:

- Be welcoming by acknowledging people waiting, listening carefully, making soft focus eye contact, and being proactive.
- Be positive in your approach and in your choice of wording.
- Watch your own nonverbal language and that of the patron's.
- Consider what library policies and procedures may be stress points for patrons.
- Use signage to prevent common irritants.
- Watch your own negative attitudes and thought patterns.
- Know what your patrons' expectations are.
- Provide patrons with a chance to provide feedback—positive and negative.
- Practice good customer service.

3 HOW TO DO IT: TWENTY BASIC STRATEGIES FOR DEFUSING ANGER

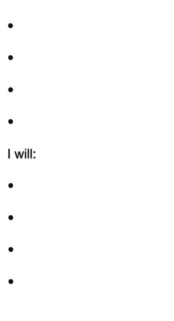

EXERCISE

THINK ABOUT IT

When an angry patron blows off steam, what are the ideal results? How do you want to conclude the encounter? Record your ideas below.

Patron will:

•

•

•

•

I will:

•

•

•

•

Coping with an angry patron is not a win-lose situation; both parties should win. Both you and the patron should have your self-respect intact. Both should feel that you've agreed on a solution to the problem that caused the patron's anger. The patron should feel better about the library both because of the way the encounter was handled and because of the resolution. And you should feel calm and in control.

This section of the book presents basic rules of coping with angry patrons. As you consider each of them, think about the exercise you did earlier in which you recalled your own experiences both with angry people and with being angry yourself.

STRATEGY 1: SET THE TONE FOR THE EXCHANGE

"It is the triumph of reason to get on well with those who possess none."
Voltaire

Greet the irate person in a calm, friendly voice, using the patron's name if possible. Typically, when a patron enters the library already angry, clearly frustrated, or looking for a fight, staff members hide. They leave the desk or busy themselves behind papers, hoping the patron will disappear. Actually, these nonverbal cues signal avoidance, which only makes the patron more angry.

By greeting the person in a relaxed fashion, you set the tone for the interaction. Keep in mind that the first speaker usually establishes the mood of an encounter. By acting friendly, you provide a pleasant atmosphere that lowers the patron's stress level as well as signaling that you expect a friendly exchange.

When you call a person by his name you are showing respect, which raises the patron's self-esteem. (For more on this, see Strategy 3.) In fact, pundits say that an individual's favorite word is his own name and that people interrupt their own thought processes and pay attention when they hear their name. Another advantage to calling a patron by name is that often people are embarrassed to be "misbehaving" (acting angry), so they hide behind anonymity which is shattered by your recognition of them. In this case, the person will try to "be on best behavior" because you know him.

A caveat about using a patron's name is necessary. As valuable as it can be, in some instances using a name can cause you trouble. Don't use the person's name in the following situations:

- if she won't know how you know it;
- if there are issues of privacy or confidentiality; or
- if you do not know how to pronounce it correctly

Believe it or not, sometimes a visibly upset patron is completely calmed by the time she begins to speak—just by the staff person's taking the initiative and setting the tone. How does staff at your library greet patrons? A simple "Hello" or "Good morning" is sufficient, though many libraries now use greetings to announce their customer service philosophy. "Hello. How may I help you today?" or "Good morning. What can I do for you?" are common approaches. The most significant element of the greeting is not the text but the nonverbal messages, so be sure to smile or nod, keep your hands calmly and quietly down, and modulate your voice to be pleasant and of moderate volume and pitch.

STRATEGY 2: BREATHE AND COUNT

"The greatest remedy for anger is delay." Seneca

A typical first reaction to an angry person is shock, accompanied by an intake of breath that is held. You should control your reaction, however, and remember to breathe. Breathing regularly and deeply (from the diaphragm) relaxes your body and increases the flow of oxygen to your brain so that you can think more clearly. Try breathing in through the nose, holding the breath for a few seconds once the diaphragm is full, and then breathing out very slowly through the mouth. Shallow quick breathing (which is the opposite of this type of breathing) is hyperventilation, which causes people to get dizzy and to faint. Remember: it is essential to stay calm or you will have two stressed-out people to handle.

"When angry, count ten before you speak; if very angry, an hundred." Thomas Jefferson.

Count to ten. This old-fashioned advice still applies when a person begins with a barrage of words, particularly ones we don't want to hear. By holding your own response, you allow the patron to vent and to calm down. You demonstrate respect. You let the person hear what he sounds like. Meanwhile, you have time to take a few breaths to calm yourself. And even more important, you don't escalate the situation by making a flip or sarcastic remark (which is like adding fuel to the fire).

By breathing calmly and postponing your response you also show that you are in control of the situation. The fact that the patron's anger has not unnerved you is a comfort to you and to the patron; the more that she is out of control, the more she wants to know that someone is in charge.

STRATEGY 3: TREAT THE PATRON WITH RESPECT

All people deserve respect and will fight for it if necessary. Since we want to minimize fighting, it is essential to show respect upfront. This allows the patron to concentrate on the issue rather than on offense or defense.

We initially demonstrate respect by giving our full attention. Full attention means leaving any other tasks while having a conversation with the patron. You and your colleagues may know that you can do multiple tasks at once and that you have lots of data to enter into the computer, many telephone calls to answer, or book reviews to read. But to the patron, continuing such tasks while he is speaking seems disrespectful. No matter how hard it is to break old habits, it is necessary to focus all your energy on the patron and show genuine interest in his situation.

Full attention also means establishing and maintaining eye contact. By "looking the person in the eye," you demonstrate both that you are paying close attention and that you are not cowed by her anger. Even if you are on the telephone or checking something important on the computer, look up and make eye contact with the person waiting in front of you. A note about "eye contact": do not make the patron uncomfortable by staring (which is looking directly into someone's eyes for an extended period of time). Instead, try "soft focus eye contact" (looking at the person's face—especially the area around the eyes—instead of straight into the eyes).

Another way we show respect is by demonstrating a belief that everyone has a right to his point of view. This is the opposite of setting up a win-lose situation where one person will be proven right and one will be proven wrong. Most disagreements center on facts, semantics, or values. Factual differences are the easiest to deal with; semantic or value differences are harder to reconcile. A patron who is asked to relinquish her seat at the Internet station to someone else, for instance, may have a different definition of "fair" than you do. Rather than argue that definition or ensure that you win, keep an open mind and prove it by listening to the patron. Show that you are willing to follow her views and opinions for awhile without making her feel inadequate or misunderstood.

Other manifestations of respect are adjusting your voice's volume, energy level, and rate of speech to match that of the patron. Matching a patron's nonverbal cues can make you seem more like the patron and therefore less threatening. And be sure to use words that the patron can understand (no jargon!).

Finally, respect implies authenticity. Simply parroting a memorized customer service phrase usually sounds phony and therefore lacking in respect. Throughout this book, sample scripts are given to demonstrate certain principles and techniques. Be sure to devise your own phrasing, though, so that you sound sincere and respectful.

STRATEGY 4: LISTEN

Although this sounds obvious and easy, most of us do not really listen to a person who is upset. It is essential to let the speaker know that you have listened and understood. The trick is to listen (not just hear) and to reply (not just absorb). Good listening is active rather than passive and responsive rather than one-way.

In addition, good listening requires understanding both the content and the feeling in a person's comments, and responding to the emotion as well as the facts.

This kind of listening validates a person's worth—everyone wants to be listened to and understood—and therefore is especially important when you are trying to calm someone. Listening well is such an essential strategy in defusing anger that the entire next chapter is devoted to listening skills.

STRATEGY 5: ACKNOWLEDGE AND VALIDATE

"Dismissing the feelings that the other person is experiencing in the moment is disastrous. You may intend the message is 'Everything will be all right,' but the message the other person is likely to hear is 'I don't understand how you feel' or 'You're not allowed to be upset by this.'" Stone, Patton, and Heen

Most of us who work in libraries are information-oriented. We like to give out information and offer solutions to problems. But an angry person is not capable of accepting information or moving directly to solutions. It is essential that you acknowledge the anger or frustration *first* and express sympathy before moving on.

There are a number of reasons for this.

- The angry patron is not ready for solutions if he does not feel heard and respected.
- Unacknowledged emotions act like static in any discussion, making it difficult to communicate. The static can block the patron's ability to listen; instead of paying attention to the staff person, the angry patron is stuck on how she feels.
- The patron may not want your solutions at all; he may just want to express his feelings and have them heard.
- Feelings left unacknowledged will disguise themselves as judgments or accusations and show up later as a misjudgment of the entire library or as a complaint to the administration.

By acknowledging the feeling and accepting its relevance, you are not necessarily agreeing with the substance of what's said or approving of any angry behavior. Instead you are accepting that the emotion is there and that it can be an obstacle to solving the problem. You are indicating that you appreciate the importance of the situation to the patron and that you are working to understand it. By showing sympathy you lower the patron's stress level and reduce any embarrassment so that she can calm down. Then you can move to fact giving and problem solving.

VALIDATING STATEMENTS

Validating statements are the way we acknowledge the emotion we hear and express understanding or sympathy. Here are some examples.

- "You sound upset about that . . . "
- "I understand how difficult that must be . . . "
- "It *is* frustrating to . . . "
- "I can relate to that . . . "
- "I'm sure this is upsetting . . . "
- "I'd be irritated, too . . . "
- "It *is* difficult to . . . "

EXERCISE

It is essential that you are comfortable with your words and don't sound like a bad actor reciting lines. Test out the formulas and then write some of your own.

-

-

-

-

STRATEGY 6: FOCUS ON THE PROBLEM

Focus on the patron's problem or on his behavior, not on the person's appearance or personality. Despite many article and book titles to the contrary, the patron is rarely the problem. The interchange you are having with the patron may be the problem. Or the patron's behavior may be the problem. Or a library's policy or procedure—to which the patron is responding—may be the problem.

Once we think of the person as the issue and label her as a "problem patron" we are more likely to:

- blame the person rather than trying to understand the situation, including the library's part in it,
- make the patron defensive, thereby escalating the situation,
- stop listening,
- be indifferent as to the outcome, or
- fall back onto our own personal attitudes and prejudices.

One way to demonstrate that your focus is on the problem is to restate it. By restating you show that you understood the situation. Note that understanding is not the same as agreeing; you can show your understanding without giving your agreement or approval. Restating also gives you the opportunity to reword, selecting your own words and eliminating any inflammatory language that has raised your hackles or may do so to the patron.

If the patron's behavior is the problem, you must focus on the behavior, state why it is inappropriate, and what the patron should do instead. For more on this, see the section on unacceptable behavior in Chapter 5.

STRATEGY 7: CONCEDE A MINOR POINT

"The more you can relieve the other person of the need to defend themselves, the easier it becomes for them to take in what you are saying."
Stone, Patton, and Heen

An angry person expects a battle. If you offer a concession—rather than a rebuttal—you appear to be flexible and conciliatory. This encourages the irate person to let down his guard, too. For example, the patron who says "I have a bone to pick with you" expects you to say "I'm sorry but I'm busy now" or "I've done nothing to you." By responding with "I'd be glad to talk with you," you present yourself as an ally rather than as an opponent. Similarly, the patron who complains about the lack of Christian fiction books on the shelf expects you to be either unconcerned or defensive about the library's selection policies. If you respond with a validating statement (see Strategy #5) the patron sees you as sympathetic and on her side. For example, the patron expects you to say "We have plenty of books; I can prove it to you if you want to see the latest fiction order" or "Very few people want that kind of book." If you say instead "It must be frustrating to find the books you want are checked out," the patron sees that you are not going to fight with her or demean her reading interests.

STRATEGY 8: AVOID RED FLAG WORDS

"There are some words that close a conversation like an iron door."
Alexandre Dumas

The vocabulary you use is the one thing you have complete control over. And words are often the red flags that cause people to become angry. So selecting your vocabulary carefully is a good place to start if you want to decrease the number of angry patrons you face.

Words, even common ones, have varied meanings to people because of the associations the words have. So the meaning of the word "devil" is dissimilar for people with different religious beliefs, and the word "government" evokes separate responses for people with different political leanings.

EXERCISE

Try this exercise with a friend or colleague if possible; comparing your answers is the most interesting part. Next to each of the words below, write down the word that is your first reaction, your free association. Then note whether *your* word is positive, negative, or neutral. Do not censor yourself, but write down that first thought.

Television

Chocolate

Immigrant

Rules

Librarian

Most people say that "chocolate" is a positive word for them. But the associated words—such as fattening, cholesterol, caffeine—are negative. So upon hearing the word "chocolate," some people have negative reactions. The word "immigrant" is neutral to many people but its associations are positive ("pilgrims") or negative ("alien") depending on geography and politics. And so forth.

The exercise demonstrates that even ordinary, seemingly neutral words can create negative or positive reactions. We can only imagine some of the responses when library staff speak of "policies and procedures" or use library jargon. For example, you say "This book does not circulate; it's for in-library use only." The patron hears "She won't let me take this book; she doesn't trust me with it." Or you say "This book is two days overdue" and the patron hears "He's calling me negligent."

Common library lingo such as "overdue fines" can make patrons see red. Sometimes referred to as the "library F word," "fine" is being replaced in many libraries by the more neutral word "charge." For instance, "I see you have a charge of ten cents on your record" rather than "You have a fine of ten cents." If you know that library vocabulary irritates patrons, by all means change it. One caveat, though. Using euphemisms can go too far; one library I know now uses "extended use fee" as a substitute for "fine" and nobody understands the expression!

One simple word that often angers people is "why." "Why" can sound judgmental or invasive. If at all possible use "how" in place of "why." For instance, instead of saying "Why did you let your overdue fines accumulate?" you might ask "How did all these fines accumulate?" A second common word to avoid is "but." How many times has someone told you "I'd like to help you, but . . . " As soon as you hear "but," you assume something negative will be said and you stop listening. If possible, replace "but" with "and." For example, instead of "I'd like to help you but I'm on the phone" try "I'd like to help you and I'll be off the phone in one minute." Or use two sentences rather than one compound sentence: "I'd like to help you. I'll be off the phone in one minute."

Other common words to avoid are "should" and "have to." Both sound as if you're giving orders (e.g., "You have to . . . ") or making judgments (e.g., "You should . . . "). Instead make suggestions (e.g., "Will you please . . .) Another red flag word is "problem"; no matter how clearly you refer to the "problem at hand," people feel that you're insinuating that they are the problem. Try substituting "Please tell me what we can do for you?" or "Please describe the situation for me" rather than "What's the problem?"

Any negative words can upset people, so phrase things as positively as possible. For example, "This is an overnight book" rather than

"When I use a word," Humpty Dumpty said in a rather scornful tone, "it means just what I choose it to mean—neither more nor less." "The question is," said Alice," whether you can make so many different things." "The question is," said Humpty Dumpty, "which is to be the master—that's all."
Through the Looking Glass, Lewis Carroll.

"This book can't be kept out the usual two weeks." Another example: "Our loan period is two weeks" rather than "You'll be charged ten cents per day if you keep it longer than two weeks." (Both of these examples of negative wording were heard in real libraries in recent months.)

Also avoid "I can't" because it sounds as if you are evading responsibility. Instead use positive words and state what you can do. (See more on this under *Positive Approach and Language* in Chapter 2.)

A final category of red flag words are the absolutes, such as "never" and "always." They not only anger people, they invite an argument on the facts of whether there are any instances that belie your statement. For example, if you say "The library never allows the public to use the staff room phone" you are tempting the patron to mention the one time an exception was made and he used the staff phone. In this case, instead of saying "never," you might say "rarely." Substitute "This often occurs . . . " for "You always . . . " Try "Perhaps you can . . . " instead of "You never."

STRATEGY 9: DON'T ARGUE

Once considered impolite, public arguments are now commonplace. As Deborah Tannen says in her book *The Argument Culture*, we live "in an atmosphere of unrelenting contention—an argument culture . . . [that] urges us to approach the world in an adversarial frame of mind." We see this in the way our society has become increasingly litigious, with lawsuits viewed as the solution to nearly all problems. We see it, too, in the popular use of war metaphors in public discourse.

From the point of view of library service, the pervasiveness of argument makes our work harder. One of the difficulties is that when people argue, their goal is not listening, understanding, and problem solving. Instead the only goal is winning, and people will do or say anything to win. When a discussion becomes a conflict, facts—and selecting the best solution—become irrelevant and triumphing over the other person becomes paramount.

One way to abstain from arguing is to listen with a goal that does not put you in a win/lose position. In other words, don't allow yourself to think in terms of battle or of winning and losing. Instead, keep your focus on the goal of solving the problem, pleasing the patron, and moving on to the next customer or task.

Remember that people tend to react reflexively to the challenge. This is a result of the "fight or flight" syndrome discussed in Chapter

"Keep cool; anger is not an argument." Daniel Webster

"There are two times to keep your mouth shut: when you're swimming and when you're angry." Anonymous

1. Social scientists say that 80 percent of people will fight back when they feel challenged. This is what Tannen calls a "a prepatterned, unthinking use of fighting." But when a patron begins an argument, staff should not argue back. We want the library to have a harmonious atmosphere; we do not want the other patrons nearby to see staff arguing with people (no matter who started it); and we do not want to model that kind of behavior as acceptable in the library. So, as Dale Carnegie said, "The only way to get the best of an argument is to avoid it."

A second method to avoid arguing is to teach yourself to ignore the reflex to fight back. If you take a few deep breaths and count to ten before saying anything, your body will assume there is no danger and will revert to its normal condition.

Many people get sucked into arguing to gratify their own egos by proving their superior intellect or vast knowledge. Others argue as a demonstration of their power over the patron to get revenge for alleged slights or disrespect. There are two ways to avoid these pitfalls. One, train yourself in self-observation so you can catch yourself before you succumb. Two, remind yourself that arguments with patrons are not personal: this is not about you so you don't need to defend yourself, prove yourself, or extract revenge.

Perhaps the most significant problem with arguing with a patron is that it implies that the issue at hand has only two sides. In fact, most library complaints, or accusations, have more than two sides. Our ability to see the many possibilities of any situation is what allows us to find mutually acceptable alternatives. In engineering, a cardinal rule is "the law of requisite variety," which refers to the necessity of flexibility in the design of machines so that the entire action of a machine is not dependent on any one part. In human terms, whoever has the most alternatives is most likely to succeed. If your friends go out for ice cream and you will only be happy with one esoteric flavor, there are few ice cream parlors you can go to and be satisfied. If, however, you like many flavors, even the corner place with three varieties can probably fulfill your wish. Similarly, in the library setting if staff have numerous ways to deal with, for instance, the request to take out a noncirculating book, there is a good chance to satisfy the patron. If, on the other hand, the only answer is "No, you may not take the book," this patron will leave unhappy. If the request to borrow a reference book is staged as an argument, the other possible solutions will never surface.

Do you have some patrons who start arguments whenever possible? Putting aside people with psychological problems or basic hostility, there are two central reasons for such behavior. First, some patrons pick fights because they enjoy the intensity, drama, and public spectacle of it. In this case a staff member should remove the stage from her. By taking the patron away from the public arena and out of sight of most, if not all, of the audience (the other patrons) the staff person is taking the fun out of arguing and making it easier for the situation to be resolved calmly.

Second, some patrons argue as a way of creating and prolonging social interaction for themselves. Studies have shown that even people with language disabilities who have trouble with other types of verbal exchange will participate in arguments as a type of social event. If you feel that the patron is lonely or disengaged from others and consistently starts arguments as a way of having social contact with staff, one way to cope with the situation is to steer the patron away from a disagreement and into a conversation. For example, "We don't need to argue about this. I'd rather hear about how you liked that book." Then if the person wants to talk for too long a period of time, the staff person can use techniques for ending any monopolization of his time. For instance, the staff member might give the patron a time limit by politely saying "In five minutes I have to return to my paperwork (or whatever) Mr. Chan." Or he might end the interaction by saying "I've enjoyed talking with you this morning Mrs. Turman, but now I must return to my other duties."

STRATEGY 10: DISAGREE DIPLOMATICALLY

Often angry patrons say things we know are factually incorrect or that we consider outrageous. The most tactful response is to say nothing at all; to neither agree nor disagree and to keep listening respectfully. But sometimes disagreeing is unavoidable. If you must object to something you're told by a patron, do so diplomatically.

Below are a number of techniques for disagreeing diplomatically. Whichever you use, be sure the disagreement is immediately followed by offering possible solutions to the presenting problem. Otherwise the discussion can become a debate over your disagreements.

FOGGING

One technique—called "fogging"—is to agree with any part of the argument you can, even if the part is minuscule. For example, an academic library patron says "This library is mismanaged. Here I have to wait in this long line to get reference help from you when there are lots of library employees just sitting around elsewhere." Which part can you agree with? You might disagree diplomatically by agreeing that the line is especially long that day, and ignoring the rest of his comment on staff assignments. If you argue, or disagree directly, the patron loses face and becomes more angry.

In another example, an angry public library patron feels that the library should pay her parking ticket after she parked at a fire hydrant because the library lot was full. After listening attentively you might say "I agree that parking around here is terrible!" You have just established common ground, an area of agreement, and you have demonstrated your receptivity.

AGREEING IN PRINCIPLE

If you do not agree with anything the angry person says, agree in principle with the statement. For example, an angry patron wants the library to ban teens from borrowing videotapes because he feels that they never rewind them. You might say "We do share a mutual concern about the care of the library's videotapes." Or "Something does need to be done about the rewinding of tapes."

SCRIPTS

Try these formulas for fogging or agreeing in principle.

- "You may be right . . . "
- "It's possible . . . "
- "You are correct in saying . . . "
- "It does sound like . . . "
- "What you say makes sense . . . "
- "That could be true . . . "
- "I can agree with you there . . . "
- "You have a point . . . "
- "That's an idea . . . "

EXERCISE

Since to be effective you must be comfortable with the phrases you use, create some of your own:

-

-

-

-

IF YOU CAN'T AGREE IN PRINCIPLE

When you can neither fog nor disagree in principle, still avoid contradicting the patron directly. Instead of denying the patron's statement, say "That's a different point of view than I've heard before" or "That's one way to look at it."

Or counter the patron's comment with a personal observation of your own. For example, an angry patron wants more evening hours and suggests closing all day on weekdays since "nobody uses the library" then. Instead of blurting out "That's not so," you might say "That has not been my experience working on Wednesdays . . . " Or just sympathize without agreeing or disagreeing: "I can see how you might feel that way . . . "

WHEN YOU MUST DISAGREE

When you must disagree, speak noncombatively. State your disagreement simply, following up immediately with a statement of interest in the patron's concern. For example, a patron who has had to wait in line might say "Why do you have computers anyway? They are always down. We should just pull them out of here and go back to the old, faster ways." In this case, you could fog by saying "Sometimes working with the computers is really aggravating." Or you might say: "I disagree; usually the computers are a great advantage over the paper and pencil methods. I can see why you're frustrated by them today, though." Or, "I see computers differently; I appreciate the way they usually speed up our paperwork. Today is really difficult, though."

AVOID "BUT"

As discussed earlier, "but" has a negative connotation. Everyone knows that "Yes, but . . . " really means "no." People stop listening as soon as they hear "but." Substitute "yet," "still," or "and" for "but" in your reply. Or make your reply into two or more short sentence without conjunctions. For instance, instead of saying "I'd like to help you but I don't have the key to that room" you might say "I'd like to help you. I don't have the key to that room. Let me . . . "

OPEN AND CLOSED QUESTIONS

All conversations use two styles of question, the open-ended and the closed. Open-ended questions such as "How did that happen?" encourage the person to talk and to elaborate on what she has already said. A statement like "Please tell me more about . . . " can be substituted for an open question. In some cultures such a request is considered more polite than a question. Closed questions that require a simple "yes" or "no" or ask for a straightforward fact such as date or name discourage further discussion. If you feel you must ask a question of someone during a disagreement in order to clarify the situation, be sure to use closed questions so you do not invite more altercation.

EXERCISE

A patron has been using the computer for a long time and many others are waiting restlessly in line. Your assignment is to uphold the posted time limit so that others can have a turn.

Patron (frustrated): "I waited my turn for the machine and now I'm using it. Everyone else can wait, just as I did."

Staff: "I understand that you had to wait for your turn. Our current policy is thirty minutes computer time per person when others are waiting. Once the others have each had a turn, you can continue."

Patron (angry): "The time limit is ridiculous. A half hour isn't enough to get things done. I have a great deal of work to do. Since when is there a law against being a hard worker? If there are so many people waiting, it means the library doesn't have enough computers. Why don't you buy more technology instead of wasting money on best-selling trashy novels and boring puppet shows? Who's running this library anyway?"

You must disagree diplomatically with the patron's statements against the library, stay calm, and get him away from the computer so that others can use it. What do you say?

STRATEGY 11: DON'T JUSTIFY

We often give explanations that are unnecessary and appear to be offered as justification or as an excuse for the situation that has angered the patron. These explanations make us look defensive.

In the previous example, a commentary on the job assignments of the other library staff would come across as making excuses for the supposed mismanagement. Only offer explanations if the person asks for them.

STRATEGY 12: DON'T USE ONE-UPMANSHIP

Do you ever find yourself thinking "You think *that's* bad? You should try this side of the desk for a change." An attitude of "I have it worse than you" or appealing for sympathy is counterproductive with an angry patron. He does not want to hear how the computer's malfunctioning causes you difficulty. He is concerned only with how the computer being down affects him.

When a patron has a complaint or problem, the last thing she wants to hear about is someone else's trouble. For example, although telling about the library's staff shortage may be your way of explaining a service delay, to the patron it may sound like "my problem's worse than yours." (Has a friend ever said to you "That's nothing! Wait until you hear what happened to me.") Similarly, comparing one patron's situation to another's can also be upsetting. For example, "All the other students manage to get to the library when they've signed up for a reserve reading hour."

Another type of one-upmanship is assuming ignorance or stupidity on the part of a patron. "You don't understand . . . " is a surefire way of angering a patron. "You should have known better" and "No one else has complained about this" are equally provocative. So is "Everyone else seems to understand that a bound periodical volume is considered a book and not a periodical."

STRATEGY 13: APOLOGIZE

If the library has inadvertently caused the anger, apologize. Do not defend the agency (or yourself) but apologize "for having caused you so much trouble" or "for the inconvenience." Don't blame the situation on someone else (e.g., a coworker) or something else (e.g., the computer) either. As mentioned above, an irate person expects you to fight back and may be deflated by a simple apology. Or he may be impressed that you have the self-confidence to admit that the library may have made an error.

Not apologizing sends a message, too. It implies that you do not care about the patron's feelings. Yet it is our job to care about their feelings if they are at all related to the library.

Keep in mind that apologizing is not the same as accepting personal responsibility for the situation. Remember the last time you were sick and a friend called to say "I'm so sorry you're not feeling well"? That friend was not taking the blame for your illness and was not saying that she caused you to be sick. Instead she was only expressing concern for your condition.

If you find it personally difficult to give apologies, it may help to couch it this way: "On behalf of the library, I am sorry that happened." For people who are allergic to saying "I'm sorry," try substituting "I wish." For example, "I wish the book you'd reserved had come in today" instead of "I'm sorry the book you reserved didn't come in today."

STRATEGY 14: USE BRIDGE STATEMENTS

Now that the patron has calmed down, it is time to move to resolution. The way you make the transition from listening and sympathizing to solving the problem is to use a bridge statement. Here are some examples.

- "Let's see what we can do."
- "Let me help you with that right now."
- "There are a few things we can do."
- "Here's what we can do."
- "Let's find a solution."
- "I'm glad you brought this to my attention."

Bridge statements signal the patron that you are now going to get to the bottom of the problem and that the discussion is changing direction. Note the use of "we" in the previous examples. "We" tells the patron that you are both on the same side (the problem-solving side) and that you are going to work together on the problem (s/he will be involved in selecting a solution). In the second example, the words "right now" underline two points: that the first part of the interchange is over and that you are not going to postpone or dismiss the patron's problem.

EXERCISE

How else might you phrase a bridge statement?

-

-

-

-

-

The bridge statement and all the other strategies discussed above fit together into a basic formula for responding to the angry patron:

Greet +

Listen +

Acknowledge +

Listen +

Apologize +

Bridge +

Solutions

EXERCISE

Think of a scenario involving a common irritant in your library. Now script out an interchange between an angry patron and yourself, using the formula on page 41.

Patron:
-
-
-
-
-

Staff:
-
-
-
-
-

Patron:
-
-
-
-
-

Staff:
-
-
-
-
-

Patron:
-
-
-
-
-

Staff:
-
-
-
-
-

STRATEGY 15: DEFINE THE PROBLEM

Although it is good to let the patron choose a solution so that she feels that she got what she wanted, it is important that the patron select from a list of alternatives that fit the library's policies and procedures. Often we paint ourselves into a tight corner by allowing the patron to specify what needs to be done rather than what she needs. The first—offering alternative solutions—is our area of expertise and our job; the second—explaining the need—is the patron's arena. For instance, a patron approaches the desk and says "That stupid copier in the reference room is broken again! I need you to photocopy this chapter of the book on the office copier for me." The temptation for the staff member is to discuss the availability of photocopiers and policies about the use of the office machine. But probably what the patron needs is some or all of the information on those pages. So the staff member should be discussing ways he can get that information. It is very possible that using the office copier is only one of a number of alternatives available.

To continue with this example, the staff person should have responded with a sympathetic statement, an apology, and a bridge statement, followed by a question aimed at discovering the patron's need. Such a response may go like this:

> "How frustrating!" (acknowledgment of patron's frustration)
> "I'm sorry the photocopier isn't working." (apology)
> "Let's see how I can help you." (bridge statement)
> "Would you please tell me what you needed from that book?" (question about need)

EXERCISE

Again, think of a scenario in which a patron demands a predetermined solution.

How would you respond, defining the problem in terms of need?

Patron:
-
-
-
-
-

Staff:
-
-
-
-
-

Patron:
-
-
-
-
-

Staff:
-
-
-
-
-

Patron:
-
-
-
-
-

Staff:
-
-
-
-
-

STRATEGY 16: USE THE SALAMI TACTIC

"If you are patient in one moment of anger, you will escape a hundred days of sorrow." Chinese proverb

When the patron's problem is complex, try slicing it into manageable pieces. In other words, maybe a patron who has initially expressed frustration with your automated reserve system then moves on to complain about how staff are not polite enough to patrons and then to the trouble she has had getting through to the library on the phone. After listening and validating, say something like "It sounds as if there are a number of things we need to address. Let's take them one at a time, okay?" Then address one small part of the problem—take the one that you feel you can solve immediately. In this case, perhaps you address the reserve issue. Sometimes the patron will leave satisfied without making you respond to the other concerns. Sometimes you must deal with each part one by one before the patron is content.

STRATEGY 17: TAKE YOUR TIME

Thinking speed greatly exceeds talking speed. The average person thinks at a rate of 600–1,200 words per minute, but speaks at an average of 125 words per minute. This means that we have a lot of spare brain power to use while listening to an angry patron.

Sometimes a patron's multifaceted complaint coupled with high emotion makes it difficult to think of appropriate solutions. If you need more time, stall by asking a question. The average person can think ten times as fast as one can talk, so by asking a question you are buying yourself some thinking time while the patron answers you.

If you need still more time, take the direct route. Say something like "I need a minute to think about how to best help you." Or even "I never thought I'd be in this situation. Give me a minute to figure this out."

Participants in workshops on defusing anger complain that "it takes too long" to interact with a patron in the ways suggested. Actually, trying to rush an interaction with an angry patron (or any patron) usually backfires and ends up taking longer. You will need to spend even more time if the patron becomes increasingly frustrated by your seeming indifference or inability. And you will need to take more time, and perhaps defend yourself, if the patron makes a formal complaint to the library administration and you are called in. So, take your time for both your and the patron's sake.

STRATEGY 18: BE ASSERTIVE

There are three basic styles of response to conflict: *avoidance*, *dominance*, and *problem solving*. In order to avoid conflict, or to end a confrontation quickly, most people act passively (submissive) or dominantly (aggressive). Neither the passive nor the aggressive person is willing to look (and listen) for a mutual solution and to work at making it succeed. This is the arena of the problem solver who understands that the best response to conflict is to move people forward to common ground.

Passive behavior is based on the hope that the problem will go away by itself.

Aggressive behavior is aimed at getting your own way, even at someone else's expense.

The *problem solver* wants open, straightforward communication that will lead to a solution acceptable to both parties. He uses *assertive* communications to avoid confusion and demonstrate self-control.

Assertiveness is exercising the right to stand up for oneself without violating the rights of others. Assertiveness is taking responsibility for one's own actions and reactions (feelings). Assertiveness is preserving the self-respect of both parties.

When you are assertive, you stand up for yourself and demonstrate self-respect. This is especially important if you feel like a victim when patrons express anger. By being assertive you also gain the patron's respect and you model the behavior you would like him/her to use in the future.

Assertive communications are characterized by:
- the use of "I statements" rather than "you statements"
- lack of blame or implied guilt
- low defensiveness
- self-respect
- setting limits

Let's look at more library examples. An angry public library patron demands that you allow both of his children (one the proper age and one not) to join the reading club. Although you are tempted to say "Can't you read the club rules you're holding in your hand?" or "Who are you to yell at me?" you decide to be assertive. So you respond with "I am sorry that you are inconvenienced by our club's age limits. I would like to help you yet I cannot while you are yelling at me. Shall we move over to that empty desk so we can talk calmly and quietly?"

Or an angry academic library patron complains about a recall notice on a book she has out. Because there are ten more days until it is due, she insists that she doesn't need to return it yet. After insulting your professionalism and the library's intentions, you would like to tell her to go away. Instead, you take the assertive route. "I understand your situation and think we can come up with some solutions. I will be happy to talk to you about it when you are ready."

Examples of assertive responses:
- "I think we should . . . "
- "I feel (emotion) . . . when . . . (behavior) happens."
- "I understand your situation yet I still want . . . "

EXERCISE

Try creating some assertive statements of your own:

-

-

-

EXERCISE

A faculty member wants a book placed on reserve, but you are unable to locate the book. Respond using calm I-statements, avoiding blame, and demonstrating self-respect.

Staff: "I'm very sorry that we cannot find the book. It must be lost."

Patron (angry): "'I'm sorry' isn't good enough. I need that book and I need it today. I've already told my students that the book will be available on reserve as of today. What do you mean you can't find it? It was on the shelf the last time I looked for it. Is the library in the business of misplacing books? I thought the library's job was to organize books so they're available to faculty and students. I'm doing my job and the library needs to do its job. What if all the faculty told the students 'I'm sorry but I can't teach today?' This is preposterous and unacceptable! Why don't you all just do your jobs!"

Staff:

STRATEGY 19: DON'T MAKE IDLE PROMISES

The angry patron assumes that you will not really care or help. All of the strategies discussed in this book are designed to convince the patron of your sincere concern and your ability to find a solution. Don't undo all of that hard work by giving empty promises or reassurances. For example,

- "Don't worry about it."
- "I'll look into it."
- "I'll see what I can do."
- "This always happens."
- "I'll try . . . "

These phrases are hollow; they offer no real promise of a solution. If the problem is such that it cannot be solved on the spot, explain to the patron what will happen next and when he can expect an answer.

Let's say that a patron is complaining about your library's loan period. He demands a longer loan over school vacation. You know that this exception can only be made by your supervisor, who has left for the day. Rather than saying simply "I'll see what I can do," you clarify what the patron wants and then make a solid promise. You might say "Let me make sure I understand what you're requesting. You would like to take this book out for the three weeks between semesters? [Patron confirms.] I need to get my supervisor's approval of this. Since she has left for the day, I will ask her about it tomorrow when we open. How can I reach you to let you know what is happening? I can call you or you can stop by anytime after 10:00."

Of course, there is one last step for any delayed response: you must follow through to be sure the situation is under control. In the example in the last paragraph, you might leave a note for your supervisor to see upon her arrival in the morning. But then you must follow through with her to be sure a decision is made and, finally, call the patron as promised.

STRATEGY 20: INVOLVE A COLLEAGUE

If you feel the heat is rising and you are becoming too upset to handle the situation well, or if you think you and the patron are going in circles without a resolution, it is time to call in a colleague. Many staff people call a supervisor in these situations—and often exasperated patrons will request a supervisor—but a coworker can be equally helpful. Essentially you need someone to relieve you and the patron needs a new calm person who may or may not be more accommodating than you are.

The direct and frank approach is to tell the patron "I think you will be happier if I ask Mr. Komatsu to work with you on this" or "I feel that we are not getting anywhere. Perhaps Mr. Harmon can be of more help. Please just wait here while I get him." If you are calling in a superior, tell the patron that. "I think that a supervisor can solve this for you; please wait while I get Ms. Schuman." Whenever possible, bring the colleague to the patron and introduce them to each other. Then summarize the situation so the frustrated patron does not get more angry by having to repeat everything you've already heard. Summarizing also gives you the opportunity to rephrase and to select the areas to emphasize. The "fresh" staff member then follows the same strategies that you have tried: being sympathetic, validating the emotion, apologizing, and listening carefully before using a bridge statement to move to resolution.

Another possibility is to call in your buddy, a colleague with whom you have made a compact to assist each other. (See Chapter 7 for more on this.) The buddy then proceeds in the manner you have already agreed on.

If you and the patron are having a serious disagreement, if you have been pulled into an argument over facts, or if the patron is accusing you of misconduct, the best approach is to call a supervisor. He or she will then take a different tack, following guidelines for managing conflict. Usually the strategy involves asking each person to explain his or her point of view and then having each person restate the other's position to check for mutual understanding before reaching a decision on what resolution is appropriate.

SUMMARY

- Coping with an angry patron is not a win-lose situation.

- Set the tone for the exchange by being calm and friendly.

- You can stay calm yourself by breathing deeply and counting to ten before responding.

- Always treat the patron with respect.

- Listen, listen, listen.

- Feelings crave acknowledgment.

- Validate the patron and express sympathy.

- The patron him- or herself alone is rarely the problem; focus on the problem itself.

- Don't fall for red flag words.

- Never argue with the patron.

- If you must disagree, do so diplomatically by fogging.

- Don't justify or appeal for sympathy.

- Apologizing shows you are on the patron's side and can move the encounter from problem toward solution.

- Use a bridge statement to move to resolution.

- Define the problem in terms of need, not solution.

- Take your time.

- Involve a colleague if necessary.

- Both you and the patron should have your self-respect intact at the end of the exchange.

4 LISTENING SKILLS

WHAT IS LISTENING?

We all listen as part of our work and personal lives. Social scientists estimate that we spend 45 percent of our waking hours listening to others. Unfortunately, though, the average person has only a 25 percent listening efficiency. This means that the average person can only recall accurately 25 percent of a ten-minute speech a half hour after hearing it.

One reason for the poor listening efficiency is the fact that our brains work so much faster than anyone can speak. The average speaking rate is 125 words per minute, but the average language processing rate ranges from 800 to 1,250 words per minute. So our brains do other things at the same time as listening; we actually distract ourselves.

Another reason for poor efficiency is that most of us listen on automatic pilot and just *hear* others rather than truly listening. Hearing requires all the meaning to be taken from the speaker's words alone, and doesn't allow for a full analysis on the part of the listener.

Fully listening includes two functions that lead to—and precede—a relevant response. These are:

- attending; and
- interpreting.

To attend to a speaker is to pay full attention. In order to do this, you must stop all other activities and focus your brain power on the speaker, using your eyes and all your senses as well as your ears. The meaning of the message is amplified beyond the words used by paying attention to body language, facial expressions, and, sometimes, to what is not said. Attending fully not only gives the listener extra information, but conveys to the speaker that her message is worth paying attention to.

To interpret a message is to make sense of it using all the cues gathered in attending as well as previous experience. Often interpreting is straightforward and easy, but anyone who has ever answered a reference question knows that "simple" messages can be deceiving. Interpreting assumes clarifying with the patron any part of the message that is unclear.

Once you understand what is said, the next step is to decide on an

EXERCISE

SELF-TEST

For each item below, mark T (true) if the description *ever* fits you, or F (false) if it *never* does.

_____ 1. When I'm bored, I feign attention to the speaker. I'm surprisingly good at pretending to listen.

_____ 2. While I listen, I have ample time to determine my response.

_____ 3. I avoid listening to certain topics or ideas.

_____ 4. I know that I "tune out" certain types of speech, accents, or styles of delivery.

_____ 5. I concentrate on the words alone, not on the speaker.

_____ 6. I try to avoid listening to certain patrons.

_____ 7. I listen only for facts.

_____ 8. I pay less attention when a patron uses certain words or phrases that anger me.

_____ 9. I am not easily distracted because I can do more than one thing at a time.

_____ 10. I usually can tell what the patron will say after I've heard the first part of the message.

If you marked any of the above with a T, be sure to read the following sections for tips on improving your listening skills.

appropriate response. Social scientists claim that it takes the average listener 60 to 90 seconds to get to this point.

BARRIERS TO LISTENING

As if the self-distraction of our fast-moving brains and the tendency to listen incompletely were not enough, many other barriers to good listening exist in the library. These include the distractions made by the noise and movement of other people and environmental factors such as the physical placement of the service desk and the lighting. But most obstacles are personal, ones we create ourselves.

We spend 70%–80% of our awake time in some sort of communication. 45% of our waking hours are spent listening.

Perhaps the most common impediment to careful listening is our belief that it is something we are naturally good at and so we don't need to pay full attention; we act as if good listening requires no effort and allow ourselves to think of other things while we listen. *Assumptions* are also widespread blocks to listening. Often we assume that we know what the other person is going to say next; we jump to conclusions based on our prior experiences. *Prejudices* and stereotyping also interfere with listening. A patron who does not speak well or has an accent, who is saying something we do not want to hear, or who doesn't look like our notion of a "serious customer," may not get our full attention. Our own *defensiveness* can also be a barrier; it is important to remember that library transactions are about the library and rarely are about us personally. Finally, certain words and phrases are *red flags* for us. Depending on our upbringing, political views, and personal opinions, we all have words that trigger an emotional response that interferes with listening.

Other common barriers are *evaluating* the speaker and telling her your diagnosis as in "What you really mean is..." *Presenting too much information* is also a trap many library workers fall into; if you give more information than the patron can handle he will be confused or you will sound defensive. *Interrupting* is another problem in that it conveys a lack of respect for the speaker.

We can eliminate these barriers by using some simple strategies.

- To keep from daydreaming or thinking about other things while listening, ask yourself silent questions or pretend that you will be required to report on what you have heard.
- To help you physically attend to the speaker, keep your body calm. For example, place your hands on the counter if you tend to fidget.

- If you tend to jump to conclusions or make assumptions, force yourself to listen to it all before responding.
- To avoid listening defensively, remind yourself that this is not personal.
- To refrain from breaking your concentration, eliminate all distractions under your control. For example, turn the computer screen away from your line of sight.
- If you find your attention is wandering, attend to the patron physically and your mental attention should follow. For example, really look at the speaker and keep your body posture erect and alert.
- To avoid tuning out someone who has a poor delivery or who has an accent, concentrate on the message rather than the style.
- To abstain from reacting instinctively to red flag words, translate the trigger word in your mind. For example, if the word "immigrant" starts you thinking about relatives who are immigrants (a positive train of thought) or if it reminds you of recent policies adopted by the legislature with which you disagree (a negative train of thought), substitute a word that is neutral to you such as "newcomer."
- So that you don't put your words (or feelings) into the speaker's mouth, try to use sentences which begin with "I" rather than "you." (See more on this in the *Be Assertive* section in Chapter 3).
- To keep information-giving to a minimum, first ask yourself "Does the patron really need to know this?"
- If you find yourself interrupting, immediately apologize and allow the person to finish.

ACTIVE LISTENING

People always need to feel listened to. In the primer on anger we discussed the importance of showing respect for the patron as a way to decrease her stress. Active listening, developed by Carl Rogers and popularized by Thomas Gordon, is the primary method of demonstrating respect for the patron.

Active listening—also called empathetic listening—is active rather than passive, responsive rather than one-way, and is sympathetic rather than judgmental.

Active listening requires careful attention to both *content* and *feeling*. If a patron, sounding harried and looking frustrated, reports that the microfiche reader doesn't work again today, a staff person who is

Research shows that most people listen at 25% efficiency. This means that, of what they heard, most people remember 25% of it correctly after listening to a 10-minute presentation. If listening on the telephone, efficiency drops to 10%.

a good listener will respond to both the emotion (frustration) and the message (broken machine). For example, the staff person may say "It's so frustrating when that machine is on the blink" before moving to a solution.

Active listening implies that listening and understanding—not responding—are the goals of the listener. That seems obvious, doesn't it? But most people use part of their brain power to figure out a response, and many people interrupt to use that response as soon as possible. In active listening, understanding the patron and confirming that you have understood are the main goals.

The basic technique of active listening is *reflection*. Reflection statements allow you to check your understanding of what the other person has said. They also allow the speaker a chance to hear back his own statements and then to refine or alter them.

By reflecting a person's statements, you also demonstrate that you have listened carefully. This is a validating experience for the speaker—everyone loves being listened to. In fact, the speaker will feel better listened to if your response is a *reflection* of what she said, rather than a solution or interpretation. In an active listening situation, solutions and interpretations should only be offered *after* you have reflected the content and the feeling of the speaker.

At the beginning of an exchange, just listen. Indicate that you are paying attention by nodding or injecting a minimal encourager such as "mm-hm." Then pause and consider what you have heard before responding. Do not judge, argue, or defend. If you need more information, ask a question using reflection. You can do that by turning one of the speaker's statements into a question. For example if a patron says "I've been to many libraries looking for this article" you might ask "You say you've been to many libraries looking for this article?" After the speaker is finished, reflect back what you have heard. (See below for more on how to do this.)

One caveat: active listening encourages the speaker to continue, to talk more, and to explain himself more fully. So if you do not want to generate further dialogue, stop using reflecting statements and move to solutions.

REFLECTION IN ACTIVE LISTENING

Rogers specified four levels of reflection:

- repeating word for word, changing only "I" to "you"
- repeating only part of what was said, using the speaker's words
- summarizing in your own words what you've heard
- summarizing content and expressing the feeling you've heard

The first type of response is *not* recommended for use with an angry patron as it may seem snide to repeat exactly. The other three types are all acceptable but the last one is by far the most powerful. By restating the content and reflecting the feeling, you demonstrate respect by showing that you understand the words of the message and that you accept that the emotion is present. Note that this does not mean that you necessarily agree with the content or condone the feeling, but that you "got" them both.

If you focus only on the possible solutions, and ignore the person's feelings, you may intensify the anger and the emotions it covers, such as embarrassment. A person who shows her anger wants to be heard and wants you to acknowledge that you have heard. (See more on this in Chapter 1.)

Here are some formulas for reflection of both content and feeling. Try these out to see if they're comfortable for you.

- "It really is _____ when _____."
  [*feeling*]   [*content*]

- "It looks like you feel _____ because _____."
  [*feeling*]   [*content*]

- "I can appreciate that you feel _____ since _____."
  [*feeling*]   [*content*]

- "I see that _____ has caused you to feel _____."
  [*content*]   [*feeling*]

A word of caution here. Avoid saying "I know what you are feeling" or "I understand what you are feeling," because an angry person

EXERCISE

Try creating some scripts of your own:

-

-

-

-

EXERCISE

A patron who has brought her preschool child to the library for story hour wants to stay with him. Although you tell her the children-only rule for children's programs, she insists on staying with her son. You politely restate the policy. She responds "I can't believe what I'm hearing! I always stay with my son during programs. The recreation department always allows it at their programs. He's far too young to stay alone! And story hour isn't crowded today; there's enough room for me."

How would you respond? Remember to listen actively: validate the patron's concerns, and use reflection statements. Your goal is to make the patron know that you are really listening and empathizing. This may take two or three back-and-forth exchanges in which she talks and you listen. Once she realizes that you *are* listening, she will calm down. Only then can you move on to explore possible solutions.

Record your action plan below:

probably will question you: "How do *you* know what *I* am feeling?" "I understand" can send the message "I've heard quite enough" or it can sound patronizing. If, indeed, you have been through a similar situation and feel like sharing the experience to prove your personal expertise, then you can say "I know what you are feeling because I've been in the same spot." No matter what wording you use, it is essential that you sound sincere; otherwise you will only make the patron angrier.

SUMMARY

- Though we spend nearly half our waking hours listening to others, few of us do so at more than 25 percent efficiency.

- Our brains work far faster than anyone speaks.

- Fully listening includes attending and interpreting.

- Assumptions and prejudices are common barriers to good listening.

- Other barriers include red flag words, evaluating the speaker, and interrupting.

- Active listening implies that listening and understanding—not responding—are the goals of the listener.

- A basic technique of active listening is reflection.

- The most powerful type of reflection summarizes content and expresses the feeling you've heard.

5 BEYOND THE BASICS: DIFFICULT SITUATIONS

COMPLAINTS

Only 4% of unhappy customers ever complains—it just seems to us like more! This means that for every 4 customers who complains, there are 94 more who are silent.

Customer service texts contend that "Every complaint is an opportunity." If a patron complains, he is giving you a second chance because he will judge the library not on the initial incident that caused the distress but on how the complaint is handled. A complaint provides a second kind of opportunity as well: a chance to fix a problem area (or stress point) that is upsetting many patrons. For every person who complains, there are twenty-four others who have the same concern but are not forthcoming.

The *Basic Strategies for Defusing Anger* in Chapter 3 apply to complaints as well. It is essential to listen carefully, sympathize with the patron's concern, and apologize for the situation. You may have to repeat this cycle—the patron may have more to say and so you have to listen and validate again.

At this point the patron should be somewhat calmed down and able to rationally discuss solutions to the problem. So you:

- *Restate* the problem the patron is complaining about to show that you understand it.
- *Ask questions* if necessary to fully understand the situation. Closed questions (one that require short answers such as "yes" or "no") are probably best. (See more on closed questions Chapter 3.)
- *Offer the patrons options* if at all possible.
- *Let the patron select the solution most agreeable to her.* Of course, since you are presenting the options from which the patron will choose, you ensure that only options acceptable to the library are discussed. You also retain control of the situation by presenting feasible alternatives.
- *Explain what will happen next.* If the problem is not something you can fix on the spot, tell the patron what you plan to do. If anyone else will be involved, tell the patron who that is. Write down the agreed-upon solution so that you don't forget—and the patron sees that you mean it. Be sure not to promise what you cannot deliver.

- *Encourage the patron to use a feedback form* if she is still not satisfied. Writing it down keeps her busy while you help someone else and gives her the satisfaction of knowing that an administrator will know of her situation. (See more on feedback forms in Chapter 7.)
- *Follow up.* If you have promised to call back, do so. If you have promised that a supervisor will call, double check that your supervisor has done so. If you promise to mail something to a patron, call her to be sure it was received. Following up on a pledge demonstrates the library's concern with patron satisfaction.

SAMPLE SCENARIO

A patron comes to the circulation desk to retrieve a book he has reserved electronically from home. The staff member checks and the book is not in.

Patron: "I don't understand. I received a postcard (telephone call, e-mail message) that the book I reserved is in. I had to leave work early to get here before you close. And now you say the book isn't in! I took personal leave for nothing!"

Staff: "I'm sorry—that must be so frustrating! May I see your library card so I can check on what happened?"

Patron (handing over card): "Here."

Staff (checking computer screen): "I see what happened. The book went to XYZ branch which is the default branch if no branch is specified. Should I have them send it over here? It will take about two days."

Patron: "Yes, I don't want to have to go to XYZ!"

Staff: "There's a couple of things we can do to save you another unnecessary trip. I can give you a telephone number to call to check on the book before you come. Or, if you prefer, I can call you when I know that it has arrived."

Patron: "I'm pretty hard to reach. Why don't you give me a number to call—but not one that gets me that electronic system that keeps you pressing numbers all day!"

Staff (handing her a slip of paper): "Here's a number that will get you directly to this desk. Anyone who answers will be able to help you."

Patron: "Thanks. But why did the book go to XYZ anyway?"

Staff: "Did you reserve this yourself by computer?"

Patron: "Yes."

Staff: "After you fill in all the blanks, the screen asks you to select a branch to receive the book. Many people don't notice that and don't select a branch. If no branch is specified, the book goes to XYZ."

Patron: "Oh . . . Well, thanks."

EXERCISE

Try scripting out a scenario from your library:

Patron:

Staff:

Patron:

Staff:

Patron:

Staff:

Patron:

Staff:

Patron:

Staff:

Patron:

Staff:

ACCUSATIONS

"Feelings are very good at disguising themselves as emotions we are better able to handle . . . most important, feelings transform themselves into judgments, accusations, and attributions." Stone, Patton, and Heen

It is extremely difficult to remember and use the basic strategies (or any strategies at all!) when faced with an accusation. No matter what the exact charges are, and whether the angry patron accuses you personally, a colleague, or your library as a whole, it is difficult to stay calm and sympathetic.

I once heard a boxer say that the secret to success in boxing is to focus on the other person at all times, even when—confronted with injury—the instinct is to think about self-protection. That advice also applies to coping with an angry accuser.

Here are some guidelines for responding to accusations:

- Concentrate on the patron and what her *need* is. This may require translating the comment into a request for service. Example: A patron says "This library never has the books I need. Who does the book ordering around here—some kind of simpleton?" Ask yourself "What would that comment be if she were calm?" Then respond to your translation. In this case, respond only to the patron's need for materials. "I'm sorry you haven't found what you need. What books are you looking for? Perhaps I can help you."

- Do not get pulled into discussion of the accusation itself and do not rationalize or defend. In the example above, avoid the temptation to discuss how book selection is done or the credentials of the librarian who does it.

- Do not respond reflexively. A typical reflexive response is to repeat the negative buzzword or accusatory label, and to defend yourself and your colleagues. In the example above, refrain from saying "Simpleton? I'm not a simpleton!" If you fall into that trap, the other library users have now heard the word "simpleton" attached to you three times instead of once.

"If you can keep your head when all about you are losing theirs and blaming it on you . . . yours is the earth and everything that's on it." Rudyard Kipling

- Don't think aloud. Instead, pause to consider your best response. If necessary, tell the patron "I need a minute to think about this" or "Wow! I never thought I'd hear anything like that. Let me think for a minute."

- Do not answer an accusation with a question; this invites more accusations. In the above example, responding with "Who are you calling a simpleton?" invites "Any of you library workers who orders the books around here must need a brain transplant!"

- Don't answer any rhetorical questions. Treat them as statements that require no response.

- Apologize easily. You can always apologize for "the inconvenience" if you don't feel you want to apologize for the named situation (in this example, the library's selection policies).

- Be positive and speak from pride. In the previous situation, you might say "Our library is proud of its collection. Among other things, we take suggestions from the public. Would you like to recommend a book for purchase?"
- Be assertive and use "I statements." It is often tempting to use "You statements" such as "You should be ashamed of yourself!" or "How dare you talk to me that way!" But avoid this reaction. Instead, speak from your point of view. For example, "I never thought I'd hear a comment like that about our library. I am proud of all our library does for the community."
- Often complainers enjoy the attention they're getting—from you and from other patrons. If you sense that this is the case, remove the accuser's soapbox. Ask him to come with you to a quieter location. Moving the patron often has the added side benefit of allowing him time to cool down. If you do not have the physical space to move far, or if you do not have enough staff to cover the desk if you leave, you can still try to remove the spotlight by speaking more softly or turning in such a way that the accuser turns too and is not as visible.

SAMPLE SCENARIO

An enraged patron is speaking heatedly and loudly to a staff member because a book is not on the shelf though the computer record says it is there.

Patron: "I just waited in line for twenty minutes, but I see lots of staff just sitting around over there. Do they only hire lazy people here or do they train you to be lazy after you're hired?"

Staff: "I'm sorry you had to wait in line so long. How can I help you?"

Patron: "It would help if more staff were working!"

Staff: "All the staff take turns working at the desk and doing other duties. Can I help you now?"

Note: Depending on whether offensive language is used, how directly personal the accusations are, and whether you feel physically threatened, accusations may be in the category of abuse. In most cases, verbal abuse is forbidden by the library's rules of behavior and/or by local ordinances. Check with your supervisor about the invisible boundary between "normal" angry encounters and verbal abuse.

EXERCISE

Try scripting out a scenario from your library:

Patron:

Staff:

Patron:

Staff:

Patron:

Staff:

Patron:

Staff:

Patron:

Staff:

Patron:

Staff:

UNACCEPTABLE BEHAVIOR

A fine line exists between angry encounters and unacceptable confrontations. A rule of thumb is that as long as the angry patron displays anger only through language (verbal and body language), library staff can follow the basic strategies. If, however, the irate patron's *behavior* is unacceptable, guidelines for staff response are different.

For example, you would follow the basic strategies with a patron who is angered by the rules for your summer reading program and *talks* to you about her perception that the policy for awarding prizes is unfair. But if that patron yells, or throws down her books, you must deal with her unacceptable *behavior*.

If the unacceptable behavior interferes with others' use of the library or threatens anyone's safety, security staff or police should be called. Check with your supervisor about the library's policies and procedures.

Steps to follow in a confrontation that you feel you can handle:

1. Make a good-faith statement. Similar to a validation, such a statement lets the patron know that you still have control of yourself and will give him the benefit of the doubt. For example "I can understand that you . . . " or "This is especially frustrating, isn't it?" Then *immediately*
2. Label the problem behavior. Example: "Shouting at me . . . " Be sure to disapprove of the behavior only, not the person or the emotion. If the behavior is not allowed by library policy (e.g., throwing materials), point that out. Then *immediately*
3. State your response. Example: " . . . upsets me so that I cannot think clearly." Be sure to use "I statements." Phrase your response so that it is clear that your reaction is counterproductive for the patron. Angry people do not care if they are causing you pain—they may even tell you directly "I don't care about your stupid headache!" But angry people *are* concerned about getting what *they* want. So in this example, you might say "Shouting at me makes it difficult for me to help you."
4. Do not allow time for patron response or discussion between the good-faith statement, the labeling of behavior, and the statement of your response. Give the patron a chance to answer after you've used the whole formula.
5. You may have to repeat the three-part formula. Give the patron this second chance.
6. Suggest a method for dealing with the anger. Example: "Why don't we move away from the circulation desk and discuss

Every discontent customer tells an average of 11 others, each of whom tells 5 others. That means 67 people are hearing negative stories about the library each time we have a complaint.

this quietly over here" or "I think it's best if someone else speaks with you now."

7. Work toward a solution to the problem by focusing on the patron's need in the context of the library's rules. Stress the positive. Example: "Let me show you an area where you can smoke" rather than "You are not allowed to smoke here."

8. If necessary, repeat the rule in question—without being defensive or apologetic.

9. Be assertive. Use direct statements that are clear, concrete, and consistent.

10. If the above methods are not effective in stopping the problem behavior, give the patron one last option: discontinue the behavior or leave the library.

11. If necessary, call the police. It is wise to prearrange a code phrase with your coworkers so that they know when you want the police to be called. For example, you might say "Please get Mr. Berman; he will know what to do." Your colleagues know that "Mr. Berman" is your internal code for "call the police."

Two other notes on responding to unacceptable behavior. First, do not use active listening in this situation. The primary goal here is to change or stop the behavior, not to help the patron feel better. Second, be aware of the strength of the words you use. The secondary goal in these situations is to gain or retain control. For example, "You must . . . " is a much more controlling statement than "I need you to . . . " or "I would like you to . . . " And both of the latter are stronger than "Would you please . . . "

SAMPLE SCENARIO

A visibly angry patron approaches the reference desk and throws down a reference book.

Screaming patron: "Everytime I come to this library something's screwed up!"

Staff: "I'm sorry you feel that way. Let's see if . . . "

Screaming Patron (interrupting staff person): "Sorry, schmorry! What about my report?"

Staff: "I'd like to help you. Yelling makes it hard for me to find solutions. If you can calmly tell me more about this, I can help you."

Screaming patron: "Something's always broken around here. Today it's the xerox machine and I have to copy this to do my report!"

Staff: "As I said, yelling makes it impossible for me to help you. Please lower your voice so we can discuss this."

Quieter patron: "Can you really do something? I have to have this information right away!"

Staff: "I have a few ideas. One possibility . . . "

EXERCISE

Try scripting out a scenario from your library:

Patron:

Staff:

Patron:

Staff:

Patron:

Staff:

Patron:

Staff:

Patron:

Staff:

Patron:

Staff:

MENTALLY ILL PATRONS OR PATRONS UNDER THE INFLUENCE OF DRUGS OR ALCOHOL

If you suspect a patron is mentally ill or is under the influence of drugs or alcohol, be wary. Clues that a person is under the influence include slurred speech and dilated pupils. (See more on this in the *Anger's Siblings* section of Chapter 1.)

To use the words of an experienced branch manager, you should "disengage and redirect." In other words, do not get pulled into a discussion of anything but a rational library need. Here are a few tips:

- Project a sense of calm—even if you do not feel it—to show that you are in control of the situation. The more the person feels out-of-control, the more important it is to him that someone is in charge. (That someone is you.)
- Do not corner or touch the patron. Often physical attacks stem from an attempt to protect personal space rather than to injure others.
- Do not treat the person condescendingly; being mentally ill or under the influence does not mean the person is stupid.
- Do not argue with outrageous statements, delusions, or hallucinations. These may be the person's reality and you must respect them as that. It is not your job to correct the person's interpretation of reality.
- Redirect the patron toward something library-related and rational whenever possible.
- Be assertive and firm—not apologetic or defensive—about issuing warnings on acceptable behavior.
- Be direct and concise in any requests or instructions. Repeat them if necessary.
- Involve another staff person so that you are not handling it alone. Beware of appearing confrontational, though, with what might appear to be a show of force.
- Walk away if you feel at risk. Be sure to stay in a visible public area; do not move to an enclosed area as the patron may follow you. Instead move to an area where there is a physical barrier between you and the patron (e.g., a desk or counter) and where there are coworkers. Listen to your instincts on this one and do not put yourself in any danger. Walk away slowly and calmly as running will only escalate a situation.

SAMPLE SCENARIO

A patron who has been wandering through the library, speaking to an invisible companion, approaches a staff person.

Patron: "That man is messing with my head."

Staff: "I'm sorry, I didn't understand you. Is someone bothering you?"

Patron: "That man behind the tree is messing with my head. Tell him to leave me alone!"

Staff: "I would be happy to help you with any questions you have about the library."

Patron (now visibly upset, voice raised): "Tell that man behind the tree to leave me alone."

Staff: "Please lower your voice so I can help you. Were you looking for a book or magazine today?"

EXERCISE

Try scripting out a scenario from your library:

Patron:

Staff:

Patron:

Staff:

Patron:

Staff:

Patron:

Staff:

Patron:

Staff:

Patron:

Staff:

TELEPHONE ENCOUNTERS

THE BAD NEWS

When unhappy, the average person remembers it for 23.5 months. When satisfied, the average person remembers it for 18 months.

Managing an angry patron over the telephone is especially difficult because you cannot rely on nonverbal cues. You cannot use your own body language to establish a comfortable climate and you cannot use the patron's body language as clues to the direction to take. Be aware that your words and your paralanguage are more important than ever during telephone calls. Social scientists claim that tone of voice, pitch, and speed of speech account for 85 percent of communication over the phone!

THE GOOD NEWS

Telephone conversations are nearly always shorter than face-to-face discussions. And many staff find it easier to be assertive and firm on the telephone than in person.

When talking with an angry patron on the telephone, follow the basic strategies as if he were physically present. In addition, try to:

- Answer the phone by the third ring. If you can't, apologize for the delay.
- Avoid a terse "Please hold," which can exacerbate the caller's frustration.
- Talk *to* the person, not *at* her.
- Set the tone for the exchange. The patron makes a decision about you—and about the library—in the first five seconds.
- Put the smile on your face into your voice. Studies have shown that usually we can tell the expression on a caller's face over the telephone! It is easy to be deluded into thinking "He can't see me rolling my eyes and clenching my fists" but the caller may still pick up on your hidden behavior from your paralanguage (see Chapter 1).
- Speak slightly slower than usual. Because the patron cannot see you—and use your body language for clues and context—she may need longer to understand your words. Do not speak slowly enough to sound condescending, however.
- If you have a high voice, speak at the low end of your register. The telephone accentuates high-pitched voices, making them sound screechier than they really are.
- Hold the receiver one inch from your mouth. Holding it closer can cause your words to sound slurred and/or to sound like you're shouting.

- Listen carefully. If the patron is repetitive or nervous, perhaps you are not listening well; these are typical behaviors of someone trying to get your attention. Remember to use "hmm" or "I see" to let the caller know you are listening.
- Avoid transferring the patron because it seems as if you're avoiding the problem. If you must transfer the call, be sure that the third party is available. If necessary, stay on the line until the proper party is found.
- If you must put the person on hold—to get information or to calm down—do not leave him on hold for longer than 60 seconds (the telephone company says 30 seconds) without giving a progress report. Always thank the person for waiting and apologize for any delays.
- If you are unable to take the time necessary to solve the problem, make an appointment to call back at a more suitable time. Be sure that the caller understands why you must call back and agrees to the scheduled time. Then call back promptly and thank the person for waiting.
- Allow the patron to hang up first.

UNACCEPTABLE BEHAVIOR

Unfortunately, many people feel that they can be rude on the telephone because they remain anonymous. Others feel that since you can't see them, it is somehow permissible to act out. If a caller behaves unacceptably you should react much as you would in the parallel situation in person; that is, you give the patron two opportunities to correct the behavior—explain why the behavior interferes with what she wants, and, if the behavior does not improve, you assertively and calmly discontinue the exchange.

If a caller screams at you, ask him "Please lower your voice. Yelling on the phone makes it hard to understand what you would like me to do." If the person continues, give a second warning by saying "Please stop yelling. I cannot help you if you yell." If the person still screams, discontinue the call by saying "I'm sorry. I cannot help you if you yell. Please call back when we can have a calmer conversation." Then hang up. An alternative script, if you know the patron's name and number—and if your supervisor agrees—is "I'm sorry. I cannot deal with the yelling. I am going to have my supervisor call you back." Then hang up.

If a caller curses you on the telephone, try this: "I really want to help you, but I'm having trouble with the language you're using. Would you please refrain from using that kind of language?" Most people will apologize and clean up their vocabulary. If not, give a second warning by saying "I'm having trouble focusing on your question (request, complaint, etc.) because of the language you are using. Please stop." If the patron continues to curse, discontinue the call by saying "I'm sorry. I cannot help you. Please call back when we can have a more civil conversation." Then hang up. An alternative script, if you know the patron's name and number—and if your supervisor agrees— is "I'm sorry. I cannot deal with this language. I am going to have my supervisor call you back." Then hang up.

If a caller threatens you physically, say "I will not listen to this; I am going to hang up now." Or "I can't help you. I will ask my supervisor to call you back." Then hang up and speak to your supervisor immediately. In some situations the supervisor may decide to call the telephone company or the police.

SUMMARY

- Treat complaints as an opportunity to please one patron and a chance to fix a problem area that also irritates others.

- When faced with a complaint, listen, sympathize, and apologize before restating the problem and offering alternative solutions.

- If a patron accuses you or someone else, translate the comment into a request for service that you can provide.

- Never get pulled into a discussion of an accusation, and don't ask questions about it.

- Do not respond reflexively to an accusation or repeat the negative label.

- A fine line exists between angry encounters and unacceptable confrontations. The difference is in the behavior.

- When a patron is using unacceptable behavior, be sure to label and disapprove of the behavior only.

- Stress how the unacceptable behavior causes a response that is counterproductive for the patron, and work toward a solution.

- If a patron will not discontinue unacceptable behaviors, be clear and assertive as you ask her to leave the library.

- With mentally ill patrons it is essential to project a sense of calm and keep a wide comfort zone for the patron. Involve another staff person if possible and walk away if you feel you are in danger.

- Coping with an angry patron over the telephone is especially difficult because you don't have nonverbal cues to help you understand the patron and you cannot use body language to communicate.

- On the phone, speak to the person slightly slower than usual and at the low end of your register. Avoid transferring an angry patron or putting her/him on hold.

6 COPING WITH YOUR OWN ANGER

Being the target of anger is extremely unpleasant. Often the anger is contagious: we become angered from handling an upset patron. A typical response to an angry patron is "Why me?" Or "How dare she talk like that to me?" Even though we know that we should not take it personally—that we should separate ourselves as individuals from our roles as library staff—it is extremely difficult to do. Even library staff who stay calm during the interchange itself may be angry afterwards.

Psychologists agree that it is healthy to acknowledge our own anger rather than to deny it or to store it up; however, "blowing off steam" is counterproductive. A 1990 statement from the National Institute for Mental Health says "People who have skills at managing their anger are less likely to suffer from emotional disorders or to be early victims of heart disease or stroke." So the question is how to release (manage) the anger in a healthy manner.

DURING THE ENCOUNTER

First of all, *breathe*. Although this sounds like foolish advice—you've probably never stopped breathing—slow, deep breathing is an excellent relaxant. Breathe in through your nose to the count of five, expanding your diaphragm as you inhale. Then breathe out through your mouth to the count of five, contracting your diaphragm as you exhale. Be sure to breathe deeply and from the diaphragm. If you're not sure how to do this, lie down and place your fingertips on your rib cage. In a lying position, we breathe naturally from the diaphragm. Note how your fingers move out on inhalation and in on exhalation. It may seem odd at first as we're often taught to suck in the stomach when we breathe in, but diaphragmatic breathing is key for athletes, singers, and actors as well as for people releasing anger. This technique can be done anywhere; it is invisible to others.

Observe the cues your body is giving you. The trick here is to catch yourself before you become really angry or upset. For example, if your thoughts are indignant or you have a desire to fight back, stop yourself; likewise if you have physical indicators of anger such as tense muscles, rapid heartbeat, or clenched teeth.

Use self-talk or internal monologue to keep your anger from escalating and to take charge of your emotions. You might say to yourself (silently) "I am not going to get angry. I will stay in control." Or "I

So you say you can't change? Every 5 days you get a new stomach lining. Every month you get new skin. And you replace 98% of all the atoms in your body in less than a year.

will not take this personally. I can better help the patron and myself if I stay calm." Or "This will pass. I can do this."

Monitor the cues you are giving to others. Imagine that you are looking in a mirror. What is your facial expression? What is your body language? Are you showing any frustration or anger? If so, you may be escalating the situation. Control your breathing and your facial expression to change the signals you are giving—and meanwhile you will calm yourself (e.g., consciously altering your expression by unwrinkling your brow, which meanwhile will relax your forehead).

Change your physical position in your chair or sit down if you have been standing. If you are leaning far forward (which is a fighting posture), lean back partway instead. If you are leaning all the way back (which can look like you're avoiding the interchange), lean partly forward (a listening position). Adjust your posture by placing your hands, open, at your sides.

Watch your paralanguage. Are you speaking in a higher pitch or volume than usual? Are you speaking faster than usual? Focus on keeping your voice calm and on speaking slowly, quietly, and carefully. Lowering your voice will often calm both you and the patron.

Try a *muscle relaxation* exercise. Ironically, the simplest way to relax muscles is to tense them first. Using your toes (since they are out of sight of the patron), tense your muscles by curling your toes as tightly as possible for a count of five and then relax them. If you can do it unobtrusively, do the same with your fingers.

Focus on the situation rather than the emotion. Ask yourself "How can I move us toward a solution to end this negative encounter as well as possible?" Concentrate on what to do instead of on the patron's anger.

AFTERWARDS

Drink cold water. It will cool you down and force you to breathe more slowly. Avoid drinks with caffeine or sugar, though, as they are stimulants.

Give yourself a *ten-second massage.* Rub your stiff neck, sore shoulder, or aching head for ten or fifteen seconds for some instant relief.

Talk it out with your "buddy" if you have one, or with another colleague or friend. "Getting it off your chest" can be a literal relief. First, express your emotions by using statements that begin with "I feel . . . " Next ask how the other person would have felt in the situation; usually this helps you to see that you are not alone in your feel-

"I know of no more disagreeable situation than to be left feeling generally angry without anybody in particular to be angry at." Frank Moore Colby

ings. Finally, use this as an opportunity to get a new perspective that might help you next time by discussing the situation rather than the emotions. Describe what happened and ask what your buddy would have done instead.

Request a *debriefing meeting*. Gathering the staff for such a meeting provides a safe and constructive outlet for you as well as a chance for your coworkers to learn from your experience and vice versa. It also gives your supervisor a chance to congratulate you and others on their good work.

Try *muscle relaxation* again, this time using the whole body. Starting with the toes, and working up the body, tense your muscles for a count of five and then relax them. Start with your toes by standing and drilling them into the floor. Then tighten the rest of the body in this order: calves, thighs, and hips; fingers, arms, chest, and stomach; head and neck. Your whole body should shake from tension as you raise your arms over your head and stretch as far as you can. Finally, relax all your muscles at the same time and feel a warmth flow through your body. The whole exercise takes only ten seconds and leaves you feeling renewed. Not only is your body relaxed, but your mind is also. A great paradox of life is that although your mind caused the body to tense, you can use your body to calm the mind.

In *Winning at Confrontation*, Arch Lustberg recommends another muscle relaxation method, too. In this one, you tense and relax your neck and head muscles. Draw your neck taut until you feel your vertical muscle and vein lines. Purse your lips and draw your jaw as tight as possible while clenching your teeth. Tighten your forehead until your eyes are barely open. Your entire head should shake. Now relax.

Rigorous exercise reduces anger and stress. Even a quick walk around the block or a series of sit-ups in the staff room can soothe body and mind. After work, any regular physical exercise—swimming, jogging, dancing—can be a stress reducer.

Another technique you might want to try is *imagery*. For this you need a quiet, private place for a few minutes. Sitting or lying down, close your eyes and breathe deeply. Then imagine yourself in a scene of perfect tranquillity. Perhaps a beautiful and serene landscape. Or a favorite place from a happy time in your own life. Hold the pleasant feelings when you open your eyes and go back to work.

Keeping a journal about the occasions of anger may be helpful. Recent medical research has shown that writing about traumatic experiences measurably improves the health of some medical patients. In one study (Goode, 1999), people in the treatment group were instructed to write down their deepest thoughts and feelings while members of the control group wrote about their plans for the day. Only the participants in the first group got the positive results. The researchers

"He who angers you conquers you." Elizabeth Kenny

suspect that "the writing task may be effective because it allows people to synthesize and make sense of their experience . . . to alter the way they think about an event, giving it order and structure." The writing measurably improved the health of patients with chronic asthma or rheumatoid arthritis—certainly it can help with stress caused by angry patrons!

Such rethinking of an incident through writing can help *change self-damaging thought patterns*. Are there certain words or behaviors that trigger your anger? Do you have irrational thought patterns? Once you understand what provokes you, you can take steps to change those thoughts. Because thinking precedes feelings, you can change your feelings, which in turn will affect your behavior.

Psychologist Albert Ellis's pioneering work on anger outlined a series of irrational thoughts that lead to anger. His sequence is "I want something (e.g., to be treated with respect). I didn't get it. It is awful and terrible not to get what I want. You shouldn't frustrate me! You're bad for frustrating me. Bad people ought to be punished." Does this model ring true?

Other forms of negative thinking that can lead to anger include:

- Blaming others (or yourself), which reflects a need for control— including placing responsibility on someone.
- Exaggerating the importance of problems or dwelling on the negative.
- Minimizing or discounting the positive, including not giving yourself credit when you do things well.
- Labeling people (including yourself) instead of their behavior.
- Seeing issues as black and white and situations as all-or-nothing.
- Predicting the outcome as negative by interpreting signs pessimistically; this can become a self-fulfilling prophecy.

Do you use a lot of blaming statements about others or "should" statements about yourself? These are often indicators of unrealistically high expectations. *Counteract unrealistic expectations* of others and of yourself by identifying them. For example, "People (or I) should know better than that." Or "Things need to go a certain way; anything else is wrong." Or "How can he think that?" In fact, it is okay for people to feel and think differently from the way we do. And it is okay if things happen in a way that we have not chosen.

High self-expectations and a need for perfection can lead to much guilt and anger. People who often tell themselves "I should have done that" or "I shouldn't have said that" create anger for themselves. Similarly, people who feel they must always be in control or must never

"How much more grievous are the consequences of anger than the causes of it." Marcus Aurelius

disappoint others often feel that they are failures after an angry episode—their own or a patron's.

Laughter is a great antidote to anger. Reread a favorite book of humor, look at those comic strip clippings by your desk, or watch a movie that always makes you laugh. As it is often said, "laughter is the best medicine."

Reward yourself for your successes. When you are able to manage your anger, give yourself a reward. Rewards not only recognize positive steps, they help people make further progress. Be sure the reward is one that is relaxing and pleasurable. To increase the enjoyment, decide in advance what you'd like to do for yourself, write it down, and make yourself a promise. To use the future reward as a tool to handle a difficult encounter, focus on the reward whenever you are tempted to get pulled in.

Reconsider your model of anger to affect your future encounters with angry people. Most of us subscribe to a model that shows direct stimulus and effect: something is said (or done) that causes the anger. But many psychologists feel that we have a *choice* of whether or not to get angry. In other words, the same words (or action) that could lead to anger do not have to make us irate. In this model, we can choose whether or not to react with anger. We have the ability to take a proactive, thoughtful course and choose anger only if it is useful to us. For example, if a patron's behavior is threatening, anger may alert us to danger and energize us to respond. But our anger is not useful if a patron vents his frustration that his time on the Internet is up; reacting with anger will not help us (or him) in this situation. In fact, anger will only cause us harm by increasing our stress and giving a negative impression of the library.

In this model, a reflexive or reactive response of anger is considered a learned response. So, we can learn to respond differently with time and practice. The process is to recognize how situations in the past have conditioned our current response patterns and to release those parts of the past we'd like to put behind us. Practitioners of this approach believe that freedom from the past means no longer being dominated by its influences, and that greater self-awareness leads to healthier ways of living in the present.

What is the one constant in every exchange you have with an angry patron? You. We may not be able to change all the library's stress points or all the users' behaviors, but we can work to change our own responses.

"To rules one's anger is well; to prevent it is still better." Tyron Edwards

"By identifying what you are doing to perpetuate a situation, you learn where you have leverage to affect the system. Simply by changing your own behavior, you gain at least some influence over the problem." Stone, Patton, and Heen

SUMMARY

- Don't take the patron's anger personally.

- During the encounter, remember to breathe and observe your body's cues.

- Use self-talk or internal monologue to take charge of your emotions.

- Try muscle relaxation during and after an angry interchange.

- After an angry exchange, drink cold water, talk to your buddy, have a debriefing meeting, and do some exercise.

- Imagery, journal writing, and laughter can help after an angry encounter.

- For a long-term approach to managing your own anger, you need to change negative thought patterns and counteract unrealistic expectations of yourself.

- Reward yourself for managing your anger.

- Reconsider your model of anger.

7 HELP IS AT HAND

Besides the techniques suggested throughout this book, there are a number of items that can be helpful to staff working with disgruntled customers. Below are some of these tools you may want to use in defusing angry patrons.

STRESS POINT IDENTIFICATION

Every library has certain policies, procedures, equipment, and so forth that consistently cause outbursts from patrons. These recurring irritants can be called stress points. Knowing what they are is essential if staff are to be well prepared.

EXERCISE

What causes patrons to be angry in your library? Check all that apply and add others based on your experiences.

___ Waiting in line

___ Circulation periods

___ Overdue fines

___ Reserve policies

___ Computers down

___ Insufficient Internet access stations

___ Requirements for getting a library card

___ Lack of change for copiers

___ Books not on shelf as expected

___ Insufficient seating

___ Overcrowded programs

___ Behavior of other patrons

___ Noncirculating materials

___ Broken equipment

___ No eating or drinking allowed

___ Other (what?):

POLICIES AND PROCEDURES

The policies of the library reflect its philosophy. Every policy must be checked against one basic criterion: does this communicate the library's values and mission? If a policy conflicts with the library's philosophy or goals, it is difficult for staff to implement. For instance, if the library is committed to serving patrons of all ages, policies should not discriminate against youth.

Sometimes upholding policy is unpopular with patrons. Although the public library is a "public" institution, access to it is a "limited right"; legal protection is available only to patron activities consistent with the library's mission. In other words, the library retains the right to define its public and delineate the services available. For example, many public libraries have different services and charges for nonresidents. Similarly, an academic library or a school library defines who it will serve and with what services; however, most people assume that it they are allowed in the door, they have the right to service. The library should have a written statement of admission and a written statement on building usage so that there is no confusion.

The library should also have written policies for acceptable patron behavior. These must focus on behaviors (not people), be specific, apply to all people, uphold the purpose of the library, apply only to conduct in the library, and include a process for appealing. Such policies should also conform to the American Library Association's "Guidelines for the Development of Policies and Procedures Regarding User Behavior and Library Usage" (1993). The behavior policies should be posted publicly for two reasons: so that the staff can point them out to patrons as necessary, deflecting the patron's attention from the staff member to the policy; and in case of lawsuits by patrons after the fact.

The Salt Lake County Libraries has created a Library Bill of Rights that is the flip side of a patron behavior policy. It delineates the behaviors users can expect from staff, such as "Library customers' complaints/problems will be resolved in 48 hours whenever possible." Since 1990, when *Library Journal* published the Salt Lake County Libraries' document, over a hundred other libraries have created such policies.

The library should also have a written policy and procedure for handling extreme and emergency situations. This should include when to call the police, what to expect when the police arrive, when to call another agency (e.g., mental health), and any legal responsibilities. A list of emergency telephone numbers and a script for calling the police should also be included.

Policy and procedure manuals should be updated regularly and be available at all service points.

THE BUDDY SYSTEM

Remember in elementary school or the Scouts when each kid had an assigned "buddy" for emergency procedures? The idea was that the two kids would look out for each other, that in case of panic there was a better chance that one of them would remember the emergency procedures, that there is safety in numbers. All of these precepts apply to grown-up library staff members as well.

Find yourself a buddy on your shift. The two of you agree to keep an eye out for each other and to be alert to difficult situations. Then you select a code word or phrase to use to alert the other. Let's say that a new resident is angry that the library requires two forms of identification to issue a library card. If the encounter escalates and is becoming extremely difficult, you say to the patron "Excuse me a moment. Sonia, coffee break time." If "coffee break" is the agreed-upon phrase, Sonia knows to come to the desk and assist you. She comes forward and says to the patron "Hello. Perhaps I can help you..." Spelling each other is a good tactic. It often slows down a patron who doesn't have the energy to stay irate very long, and it buys the initial staff person time to calm down. If nothing else, the buddy's arrival is a show of strength ("safety in numbers") and a witness if things get out of control.

The buddy is also the person you talk to after an unpleasant situation. She agrees to listen to you as you gripe about it and you agree to let her make suggestions to improve your performance next time. Many staff members find that having a buddy is like insurance; they rarely use it but feel better for having it.

TEAMWORK

In addition to a buddy, every public service staff person should feel comfortable asking for assistance from another. Many times an angry patron will ask to speak to "the supervisor" or "the person in charge." Supervisors should be sure that staff members know when to call him or her; often the fact of speaking to "the boss" pleases patrons. A caution here: the angry patron may act completely different with the supervisor than with the employee. Sometimes this is to impress the supervisor, other times it is just because the patron has had the time and opportunity to calm down before seeing the supervisor.

Whether the patron asks for a supervisor or not, finding another staff person to assist is often a wise choice. If you find that you are getting upset yourself, or if you simply feel that you are making no progress with the patron, involve a coworker. Since the angry person wants to be heard—and to be helped—getting another staff member involved is usually seen as a positive step. Sometimes, though, people become more angry, especially if they feel they are being "passed around" or that staff is avoiding the situation. So be diplomatic in getting assistance.

You might say to the user "I don't seem to be able to satisfy you; let me find someone who can help." Or "Why don't I get someone else who may be able to solve this for you. Please wait just a moment." Then find a coworker and fill him in on the situation so that the patron does not have to repeat everything. The coworker introduces himself to the patron and says something like "I understand that there's a discrepancy in our records. Let's see what I can do to clear this up." If necessary, he can ask a question to clarify the situation. Colleagues and supervisors should never criticize the initial staff member to the patron, but should pick up from where that person left off.

INCIDENT REPORTS

The most important follow-up to any encounter with an angry patron is the incident report. Most libraries have incident report forms for use when the police or security is called, but similar forms should also be used for every event of anger or confrontation.

The form should include the date and time, the staff person's name, the patron's name (if known), a physical description of the patron, the presenting problem (e.g., upset that the library no longer keeps a reading record of all the materials she has checked out during the last year), and the resolution. The form should be filled out by any and all staff members involved (not by a supervisor) and turned in to the supervisor with a copy to security (if the library has such). In a large library or system, these forms should be faxed to an administrator assigned to handle them so that immediate feedback can be given to the staff members involved and, when necessary, branches can be alerted to situations as they develop.

In some libraries this type of information is entered and kept as a computer record rather than a paper hard copy. This way, staff members can pull up files to determine whether, for example, a patron has a legitimate complaint or is a habitual complainer. For example, a patron who brings an overdue notice to the desk along with a book he claims to have found on the shelf may have caught a staff error (book shelved but not wanded in) or may be using a common tactic to avoid overdues. Other libraries have determined that such a computer file leaves the library open to lawsuits.

Whether paper or electronic, incident forms are extremely useful for a number of reasons:

- A chance to "get it off your chest" for the staff person involved; this is especially significant if there is no buddy system.
- Basis of future training; common scenarios can be used to train new or existing staff in defusing anger and handling complaints.
- Record of difficult patrons to alert other staff; if the same person habitually exhibits problem behaviors, a plan of action can be developed.
- Consideration of policy or procedure changes; if certain policies or procedures often upset patrons, the library administration and board should be alerted.
- Information for the library board and/or city council; a composite portrait of the year's incidents can assist the powers that be to view the library (and its staffing needs) realistically.
- Document the need for security staff.
- Provide documentation for the police and/or court system should legal action become necessary.
- Ensure that supervisors have the information necessary to support and congratulate staff for their work.

SAMPLE INCIDENT REPORT FORM

Date and time: _____

Location (i.e., department): _____

Initial staff person: _____

Other staff involved: _____

Patron name (if known): _____

Patron description:

Issue (i.e., stress point):

Resolution:

Notes (e.g., what the library might do to affect this stress point; what the staff person might do differently next time; request for follow-up by staff member):

REBUTTAL FILES

Commonly used by salespeople, a rebuttal file is a series of scripts for answering the most common complaints. Though no one should simply read a script to an angry (or any) patron, writing out possible responses ahead of time can be good preparation.

This is best done as a group activity. All the staff in a department or unit meet and brainstorm alternative answers to patrons who are upset by a specific stress point. These scripts are then presented in role plays so that all participants can see how they will "play out." After more discussion on them, the responses are rewritten and retried until the staff members feel comfortable with the various possibilities for that stress point. And so on.

Scripting and practicing rebuttals not only increases staff's confidence about dealing with difficult situations but assures that staff responses are reasonably consistent.

CHEAT SHEETS

Cheat sheets are quick reference guides kept at the service desks for staff to remind them of basic points to make or a rebuttal script to use if they are stymied during an exchange with an angry patron. Libraries should make their own based on the policies and procedures of the library as well as the common stress points. An example is on the following page.

SAMPLE QUICK REFERENCE GUIDE

With an Angry Patron

- Breathe.
- Don't take it personally.
- Listen first.
- Show sympathy for the situation. "It is frustrating to . . . "
- Don't justify.
- Don't argue. "That's a possibility."
- It's okay for the patron to feel differently than you do. "You may be right."
- Watch your body language.
- Talk to yourself. "I can handle this. This is not about me."
- Offer options. "Here are some things we can do."
- Call in a coworker to help you.

With Unacceptable Behavior

- Show good faith.
- Label the behavior (not the person).
- State your response to the behavior.
- Suggest alternatives.
- Be clear and assertive.
- If the behavior persists, call security.

BIBLIOGRAPHY

Aguilar, Leslie, and Linda Stokes. *Multicultural Customer Service: Providing Excellent Service across Cultures.* New York: Irwin Books, 1996.

Arterburn, Tom R. "Librarians: Caretakers or Crimefighters?" *American Libraries* 27(7): 32–34, August 1996.

Axtell, Roger E. *Gestures: The Dos and Taboos of Body Language around the World.* New York: Wiley, 1991.

Bach, George R., and Herbert Goldberg. *Creative Aggression.* New York: Avon Books, 1974.

Bolton, Robert. *People Skills: How to Assert Yourself, Listen to Others, and Resolve Conflict.* New York: Touchstone Books (Simon & Schuster), 1979.

Bramson, Robert. *Coping with Difficult People...In Business and In Life.* New York: Ballantine Books, 1981.

Caputo, Jeanette S. *The Assertive Librarian.* Phoenix: Oryx Press, 1984.

Comstock-Gay, Stuart. "Disruptive Behavior: Protecting People, Protecting Rights." *Wilson Library Bulletin* 69(6): 23–25, February 1995.

Conroy, Barbara, and Barbara Schindler Jones. *Improving Communication in the Library.* Phoenix: Oryx Press, 1986.

Elgin, Suzette Haden. *The Gentle Art of Self-Defense Workbook.* New York: Dorset Press, 1987.

———. *The Gentle Art of Verbal Self-Defense.* New York: Prentice-Hall, 1980.

Ellis, Albert. *Anger: How to Live with It and without It.* Secaucus, N.J.: Citadel Press, 1977.

Folger, J., and M. Poole. *Working Through Conflict: A Communication Perspective.* New York: Scott, Foresman, and Co., 1984.

Goode, Erica. "Can An Essay A Day Keep Asthma or Arthritis at Bay?" *New York Times,* April 14, 1999.

Leland, Karen, and Keith Bailey. *Customer Service for Dummies.* Foster City, Calif.: IDG Books, 1995.

Lerner, Harriet Goldhor. *The Dance of Anger.* New York: Harper, 1985.

"Library Bill of Rights." *Library Journal* 115(6): 30, April 1, 1990.

Luhn, Rebecca R. *Managing Anger.* Los Altos, Calif.: Crisp Publications, 1992.

Lustberg, Arch. *Controlling the Confrontation.* Chicago: ALA, 1993. (Audiotape or videotape)

———. *Winning at Confrontation.* Washington, D.C.: U.S. Chamber of Commerce, 1993.

Matthews, Anne J. *Communicate: A Librarian's Guide to Interpersonal Communications.* Chicago: ALA, 1983.

McNeil, Beth, and Denise J. Johnson. *Patron Behavior in Libraries: A Handbook of Positive Approaches to Negative Situations.* Chicago: ALA, 1996.

Miller, Dennis. "An Attitude of Caring." *The Reference Librarian* 60: 139–144, 1998.

Morgan, Rebecca L. *Calming Upset Customers: Staying Effective during Unpleasant Situations.* Los Altos, Calif.: Crisp Publications, 1989.

Owens, Sheryl. "Proactive Problem Patron Preparedness." *Library and Archival Security* 12(2): 11–23, 1994.

Ross, Catherine Sheldrick, and Patricia Dewdney. *Communicating Professionally: A How-To-Do-It Manual for Librarians.* 2d edition. New York: Neal-Schuman Publishers, 1998.

Rubin, Rhea Joyce. "Anger at the Reference Desk (and Elsewhere)" in Katz, Bill, editor. *The Reference Library User.* New York: Haworth Press, 1990, pp. 34–52.

Salter, Charles A., and Jeffrey L. Salter. *On the Frontlines: Coping with the Library's Problem Patrons.* New York: Libraries Unlimited, 1988.

Shuman, Bruce. "Designing Personal Safety into Library Buildings." *American Libraries* 27(7): 37–39, August 1996.

———. *River Bend Revisited: The Problem Patron in the Library.* Phoenix: Oryx Press, 1984.

Smith, Kitty. *Serving the Difficult Customer: A How-To-Do-It Manual for Library Staff.* New York: Neal-Schuman Publishers, 1993.

Smith, Nathan M., and Irene Adams. "Using Active Listening to Deal with Patron Problems." *Public Libraries* 30(4): 236–239, July/August ,1991.

Stone, Douglas, Bruce Patton, and Sheila Heen. *Difficult Conversations: How to Discuss What Matters Most.* New York: Viking Penguin, 1999.

Tannen, Deborah. *The Argument Culture: Stopping America's War of Words.* New York: Ballantine Books, 1999.

Tavris, Carol. "Anger Defused." *Psychology Today* 16 (11): 25–34, November 1982.

———. *Anger: The Misunderstood Emotion.* New York: Touchstone Books (Simon & Schuster), 1982.

Turman, Janet. "Managing Difficult Situations in Public library Service: A Continuing Process." Workshops in California, 1998.

———. "Managing Difficult Situations in Public Library Service: Procedures and Communication Skills for Supervisors." Presentation at the California Library Association, 1998.

Turner, Anne M. *It Comes with the Territory: Handling Problem Situations in Libraries.* Jefferson, N.C.: McFarland and Co., 1993.

Walters, Suzanne. *Customer Service: A How-To-Do-It Manual.* New York: Neal-Schuman Publishers, 1994.

Weisinger, Hendrie. *Dr. Weisinger's Anger Workout Book.* New York: Quill Press, 1985.

Wells, T. *Keeping Your Cool Under Fire.* New York: McGraw-Hill, 1980.

Weyant, Bob. *Confrontation without Guilt or Conflict.* Bellevue, Wash.: Brassy Publishing, 1994.

Willis, Mark R. *Dealing with Difficult People in the Library.* Chicago: ALA, 1999.

INDEX